Footsteps

NUMBER THIRTY-EIGHT

The Centennial Series of the Association of Former Students, Texas A&M University

Footsteps

A GUIDED TOUR
OF THE
TEXAS A&M UNIVERSITY
CAMPUS

By Jerry C. Cooper
and
Henry C. Dethloff

Texas A&M University Press
College Station

LIBRARY OF CONGRESS CATALOGING-IN-PUBLICATION DATA

Cooper, Jerry C., 1941–
       Footsteps : a guided tour of the Texas A&M University campus /
by Jerry C. Cooper and Henry C. Dethloff.
       p.   cm. – (The Centennial series of the Association of
Former Students, Texas A&M University ; no. 38)
       Includes index.
       ISBN 0-89096-459-9. – ISBN 0-89096-462-9 (pbk.)
       1. Texas A&M University–Guidebooks.   I. Dethloff, Henry C.
II. Title.   III. Series.
LD5309.C66 1991
378.764′242–dc20
                                                                    90-40744
                                                                        CIP

To the memory of
   MARION THOMAS HARRINGTON '22,
   president and chancellor of Texas A&M,
   who devoted his life to his school

Contents

Acknowledgments   *page* ix
List of Sites   xi
Introduction   xv

Tour A. Alumni to Athletics
Clayton W. Williams, Jr., Alumni Center (A1) to
Albritton Bell Tower (A17). Distance: 1.7 miles   3

Tour B. The West Campus
Start and end at Albritton Bell Tower (A17).
Distance: 1.5 miles   41

Tour C. The Traditional Campus
Albritton Bell Tower (A17) to Rudder Tower (A7).
Distance: 1.1 miles   59

Tour D. Cadets to Computers
Rudder Tower (A7) to System Administration
Building (D21). Distance: 1.4 miles   93

Tour E. Old Meets New
System Administration Building (D21) to
Rudder Tower (A7). Distance: 1.5 miles   127

Afterword   162
Index   163

Acknowledgments

A book such as this may be authored by only a few individuals, but in truth it is through the combined efforts of many that its publication is possible. Some of those we thank are Anthony J. ("Tony") Heger (Class of 1961), A&M Facilities Administration Division manager, for invaluable details and dates on campus construction and renovation; Paul M. Glenn and Elizabeth ("Libby") Basham of A&M Photographic Services, and Glen Johnson (Class of 1978) of Johnson Photography for helping put together the photograph collection; Deborah Partain, manager of the Cartographic Services Unit of the College of Geosciences, for preparing the maps; and Harvey R. Striegler, Jr. (Class of 1964), A&M associate director for admissions, for permitting us to adapt the campus map prepared for his office.

David L. Chapman (Class of 1967), A&M associate archivist, provided early assistance in locating materials and walked a few of the preliminary routes. John A. Adams, Jr. (Class of 1973), read early versions of the manuscript and made many useful suggestions.

We also thank W. G. ("Glen") Dowling, A&M director of planning and institutional analysis, for his gracious help in defining current and historical uses of campus buildings, and John M. Norris (Class of 1984), director of A&M's international coordination office, and John J. Koldus, A&M vice president for student services, for reviewing the manuscript and providing helpful suggestions.

Finally, we would like to thank the many other people who read the manuscript, took photographs, tested the tours, and contributed countless hours toward making this book as complete, attractive, and accurate as possible.

Photography credits are keyed as follows:

DG	Derrick Grubbs
CA	College of Architecture
GJ	Glen Johnson Photography
JC	Jerry Cooper
MB	Mack Bradford
NP	Noel Parsons
PS	Photographic Services
TA	*The Texas Aggie*

Sites

Tour A: Alumni to Athletics

A1.	Clayton W. Williams, Jr., Alumni Center	*page* 3
A2.	University Police Headquarters and Project House Site	6
A3.	Moore Communications Center	7
A4.	Floral Test Garden and Texas A&M Armillary Sphere	8
A5.	President's Home	9
A6.	Sanders Corps of Cadets Visitor Center	12
A7.	Rudder Tower and Theater Complex	12
A8.	Simpson Drill Field	16
A9.	Memorial Student Center	18
A10.	G. Rollie White Coliseum	24
A11.	Twelfth Man Foundation and Twelfth Man Statue	26
A12.	Kyle Field and Steed Conditioning Laboratory	27
A13.	DeWare Field House, Downs Natatorium, Cain Pool, and the West Side Athletic Complex	31
A14.	Board of Regents' Annex	34
A15.	Cain Athletic Hall	35
A16.	The Grove	35
A17.	Albritton Bell Tower	36

Tour B: The West Campus

B1.	West Gate	41
B2.	Kleberg Animal and Food Sciences Center	43
B3.	Heep Center for Soil and Crop Sciences	45
B4.	Rosenthal Meat Science and Technology Center	45
B5.	Biochemistry/Biophysics Building	47
B6.	Horticulture and Forest Science Building	49
B7.	Reynolds Medical Sciences Building and the Medical Sciences Library	50
B8.	Texas Veterinary Medical Center	52
B9.	Eli Whiteley Park	55
B10.	Agricultural Engineering Shops	56
B11.	Cater-Mattil Hall	56

Tour C: The Traditional Campus

C1.	Old Main Drive	59
C2.	Henderson Hall	59
C3.	Law and Puryear Halls	61
C4.	Coke Building	62
C5.	YMCA Building	63
C6.	Beutel Health Center	65
C7.	All Faiths Chapel	65
C8.	Lechner, McFadden, and Haas Halls	67
C9.	Fish Fountain	69
C10.	Special Services Building	69
C11.	Sbisa Dining Hall	70
C12.	North Dorm Area	72
C13.	Bell Building	74
C14.	Hobby, Neeley, and Hotard Halls	74
C15.	Military Walk	75
C16.	Legett Hall	76
C17.	Milner Hall	77

C18.	Heaton Hall	78
C19.	Fermier Hall	78
C20.	English Annex	80
C21.	Thompson Mechanical Engineering Shops	80
C22.	Harrington Education Center and Annex	81
C23.	Bolton Hall	82
C24.	Academic Building	83
C25.	Nagle Hall	88
C26.	Hart Hall	89
C27.	Bizzell Hall	90

Tour D: Cadets to Computers

D1.	Military Sciences Building	93
D2.	Psychology Building	95
D3.	Butler Building	95
D4.	Analytical Services Building	97
D5.	Heldenfels Hall	97
D6.	Corps Dorm Area	98
D7.	Duncan Dining Hall	102
D8.	Adams Band Hall	104
D9.	Lindsey Building	104
D10.	Aggie Bonfire (Duncan Field)	106
D11.	Modular Dormitories	108
D12.	The Commons	109
D13.	Texas Agricultural Experiment Station Annex	111
D14.	Golf Course and Clubhouse	113
D15.	Teague Research Center and Computing Services Complex	113
D16.	Beasley Laboratory and Greenhouses	115
D17.	Herman F. Heep Building	116
D18.	The Pavilion	116

D19.	Animal Industries Building	117
D20.	Eller Building	121
D21.	System Administration Building	121

Tour E: Old Meets New

E1.	Langford Architecture Center	127
E2.	Scoates Hall	129
E3.	Aerospace Engineering and Computer Science Building	131
E4.	Wisenbaker Engineering and Research Center	132
E5.	Civil Engineering Building	133
E6.	Richardson Building	134
E7.	Doherty Building	137
E8.	Civil Engineering/Texas Transportation Institute Building	137
E9.	Zachry Engineering Center	139
E10.	Cyclotron	141
E11.	Engineering/Physics Building	141
E12.	Halbouty Geosciences Building	143
E13.	Blocker Building	146
E14.	Northside Parking Garage and Power Plant Area	146
E15.	Printing Center and Reed McDonald Building	148
E16.	Chemistry Complex	149
E17.	Francis Hall	152
E18.	Engineering Building	153
E19.	Evans Library	155
E20.	Agriculture Building	157
E21.	Peterson Building	158
E22.	Biological Sciences Building	159
E23.	Cushing Library Wing	160

Introduction

Texas A&M University began serving the people of Texas and the nation in 1876 and was Texas' first public institution of higher education. The "campus" at that time was a tangle of dewberry bushes, weeds, and brush on a rise some four miles south of the raw frontier town of Bryan, itself founded just five years earlier. The City of College Station would not be founded until sixty-two years later.

Much has changed since then. The main campus of Texas A&M University, the heart of Aggieland, covers an area of approximately 1.5 square miles. On the campus are nearly 250 buildings and other structures that serve a student, faculty, and staff population of more than 46,000 people, a fair-sized city in itself.

Visitors are always welcome at A&M, and one of the oldest and best Aggie traditions is a smile, a "howdy," and an offer of assistance to guests. The Campus Information Center is located on the ground floor of Rudder Tower (A7), but don't hesitate to ask any passing student or stop by any campus office for information or directions if you need help.

Parking

Visitors are asked to park only in lots designated for their use and to ride the on-campus shuttle buses, which stop at convenient locations throughout campus.

Visitors who bring their cars on campus for conferences and other official business are invited to park in Lot 48 just south of the east wing of Kyle Field (A12) until a new parking garage with space for visitors is opened south of Rudder Tower and Theater Complex (A7) in late 1991 or early 1992. Visitor parking is also available in the North-side Parking Garage (E14) on University Drive.

Other parking areas on campus are open to visitors with temporary parking permits. Permits and information on parking can be obtained from the university's Department of Parking, Transit, and Traffic Services in the Southwest Savings Building at 717B University Drive just north of the Blocker Building (E13). Visitors should be aware that they are not exempt from fines for improper parking in fire zones or restricted areas and are subject to having their vehicle towed at their expense.

How to Use This Guide

Because of the size of the A&M campus, this guide is divided into five different walking tours, each covering a distinct section of the campus. A map of each section, with the tour marked by a line and arrows, is included on the following pages, and directions printed in bold italics within the tour descriptions give information on turns and locations.

Texas A&M was originally laid out to parallel the rail-road tracks, and as a result, none of the campus streets runs truly north-south or east-west. For the purposes of this guide, however, directions will be given as if the streets parallel to the tracks run north-south and streets perpendicular to the tracks run east-west. The compass roses on the maps in this book are turned slightly to indicate those directions rather than true north.

You can begin your exploration of the campus at any number of points: the Clayton W. Williams, Jr., Alumni Center (Tour A); the Albritton Bell Tower (Tours B and C); Rudder Tower (Tour D); the System Administration Building (Tour E), or any point in between. To begin a tour at a place other than the starting point, simply identify a nearby building in the index, which will provide the location number of that building in your tour book, then follow the map and the bold italicized directions to continue the tour from that point. Because the campus is constantly growing and changing, some of the tour routes printed in this book may be blocked by new construction. To find a suitable detour, simply take note of where the tour is interrupted on the map and circle the construction until you can pick up the route again.

The approximate walking distance of each tour is indicated at the start of the tour. None of the tours, as described, is longer than two miles.

The photographs in the book, selected to show prominent landmarks or features of their detail, can also be used to locate your place along a tour. You might also enjoy comparing the present views of campus with historical images of many of the same scenes in the book *A Pictorial History of Texas A&M University, 1876–1976*, by Henry C. Dethloff, available from local bookstores and the University Press (D9).

These tour directions should be considered only an introduction to the fascinating sights that can be yours with a little additional exploration. Many of the campus buildings mentioned in this book have interesting features that, for reasons of limited space, could not be described here, and almost all of them, except residences, have lobbies, hallways, and other public areas that are open during regular business hours. Don't be afraid to take side-trips off the marked routes, for there are many nooks and crannies of campus that will reward the curious walker with an interesting bit of architecture or at least a quiet, shady spot to pause and reflect on the footsteps that have passed that way before.

Important Telephone Numbers

As dialed from all on-campus 845 and 847 exchange telephones:

Emergency	9-911
Association of Former Students	5-7514
Campus Directory Assistance	5-3211
Campus Information Center, Rudder Tower (A7)	5-5851
On-Campus Shuttle Bus Information	5-1971
Parking, Transit, and Traffic Services	5-9700
Student Locator	5-4741
University Police (nonemergency)	5-2345

Footsteps

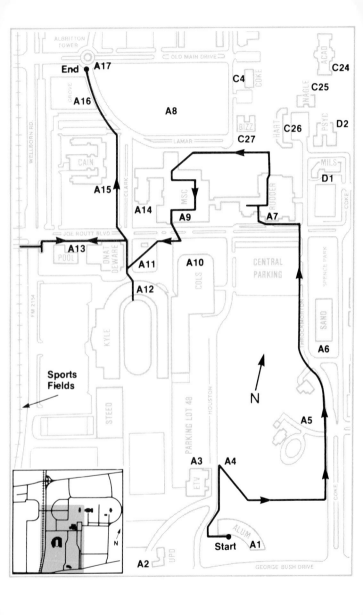

Tour A

Alumni to Athletics: Clayton W. Williams, Jr.,
Alumni Center to Albritton Bell Tower (Distance:
1.7 miles)

*Begin the tour by exiting the Clayton W. Williams, Jr.,
Alumni Center through its front entrance and bearing to
the right toward Houston Street.*

A1

Clayton W. Williams, Jr., Alumni Center

Texas A&M University's alumni center is named for Distinguished Alumnus Clayton W. Williams, Jr. (Class of 1954). The center, which opened in the fall of 1987, is the first permanent home of the Association of Former Students, which began as the Association of Ex-Cadets in 1879. The Ex-Cadets were reorganized in 1886 as the Alumni Association, from which was born the present association in 1919. Records are maintained on more than 150,000 former students of Texas A&M.

The Association of Former Students was previously housed in the James ("Scotty") Forsyth Alumni Center, located in the Memorial Student Center. Before that the offices were in the YMCA Building, and in the System Administration Building.

The new Alumni Center reflects the size and prestige

3

Clayton W. Williams, Jr., Alumni Center (A1) *JC*

of one of the largest alumni associations in the United States. The Association of Former Students and the equally unique Federation of Texas A&M University Mothers' Clubs provide current students and faculty with enormous financial and moral support. Each year former students and friends of Texas A&M contribute more than $4 million to the association's Annual Fund. The association runs one of the largest class reunion programs in the world, has helped establish more than three hundred local A&M Clubs, and provides funding for numerous faculty/staff and student awards.

The Alumni Center houses the Josh Sterns Collection of A&M College Rings and the Memorial University Ring Collection along with a number of class rings that are unique or that belonged to former students who were significant in Texas A&M's history. In the Hall of Honor are plaques noting the accomplishments of more than a hundred individuals who have been presented the Distinguished Alumnus Award and more than 150 Aggies who have achieved flag rank in the military services.

Gracing the plaza in front of the building is the passive-flow fountain dedicated in 1989 to Henry A. Hansen (Class of 1942) by his three Aggie sons. The fountain consists of 336 separate pieces of carnelian granite weighing a total

Interior of Alumni Center (A1) *PS*

of thirty-one tons. The ninety-six keystones were placed at precisely the same elevation to enable the fountain to flow properly. The centerpiece of the fountain, a gift of the Class of 1955, is a forty-two-piece sculpture of the Association of Former Students' official seal on a sunburst pedestal. The entire sculpture weighs ninety-five tons.

A2

University Police Headquarters and Project House Site

As you walk past the Hansen Fountain in front of the Alumni Center, look across Houston Street at the University Police headquarters. The enlarged building includes one of the last remaining "project houses," inexpensive housing for students during and after the Great Depression.

Cooperative housing began on the A&M campus in 1932. In that year Dan Russell, a professor of rural sociology, was authorized by the Board of Directors (now the Board of Regents) to sponsor a house where twelve boys could live and do their own cooking and cleaning. One boy brought two milk cows, and each was required to bring four laying hens. They bought their groceries wholesale. The experiment was so successful in enabling boys to continue their education in the midst of hard times that in 1936 the board approved a comprehensive "project" house or cooperative student housing program, and by the end of 1937 there were over fifty student cooperative houses on and adjacent to the campus. Russell estimated that the average household expense of a student living in the cooperatives in 1938 was $13.34 per month.

The land behind the police headquarters was occupied from 1937 until 1988 by Southside Apartments, a number of wood, lap-sided, two-story apartments built as student cooperative housing and more recently used for married student housing.

Turn right and proceed north on Houston Street, named for A&M President David Franklin Houston, 1902–1905, who later became Woodrow Wilson's secretary of agriculture.

A3

Moore Communications Center

The beginnings of the Moore Communications Center, which houses Texas A&M's public radio (KAMU-FM) and television (KAMU-TV) stations, can be traced to a small, student-built wireless station, 5YA, located in the Electrical Engineering Building (Bolton Hall, C23). On November 24, 1921, during the annual gridiron contest between the University of Texas and Texas A&M, this station made radio history by broadcasting (in Morse code) the first play-by-play account of a football game.

The following year, Texas A&M established radio station WTAW, the first in central Texas. The call letters, selected by student vote, stand for *Watch The Aggies Win.* Although the station was sold in 1958, many students were trained in radio communications there, and because of its successes Texas A&M became deeply committed to the use of electronic media in education.

As early as 1953, the university reserved an educational television channel, and in 1965 it began broadcasting classroom instruction. From the first TV station in old Bagley Hall, where the Harrington Education Center (C22) now stands, the infant educational enterprise was soon producing over 100,000 credit hours of classroom viewing annually. On February 15, 1970, KAMU-TV (Channel 15) went on the air, and in March, 1972, the station moved into its new home in the Moore Center. KAMU-FM (90.9 MHz) began broadcasting March 31, 1977.

The center is named for Austin and Midland geologist Joe Hiram Moore (Class of 1938), a Distinguished Alumnus of Texas A&M University, a former president of the Association of Former Students, and a former chairman of the Texas A&M University Development Foundation Board of Trustees.

A4

Floral Test Garden and Texas A&M Armillary Sphere

Maintained by the Horticultural Sciences Department of the College of Agriculture, the Floral Test Garden shows off colorful floral plants chosen to suit the season and to reflect developments in plant selection and breeding. The garden was the idea of A&M President James Earl Rudder and was first planted in 1969. It exhibits as many as two hundred to three hundred floral varieties in a year.

Between Houston Street and the Floral Test Garden is the Texas A&M Armillary Sphere. This unusual device, an elaborate sundial, shows the carefully calculated "sun time" for Texas A&M University. As the inscription explains, sun time is twenty-six minutes slower than clock time. The instrument was donated by Houston attorney and A&M Distinguished Alumnus Searcy Bracewell (Class of 1938).

From the Floral Test Garden you may notice the jogging trail that loops one mile through the campus grounds.

Follow the jogging path behind the Alumni Center (A1) south and eastward from the Floral Test Garden to Throck-

Armillary Sphere in the Floral Test Garden (A4) *PS*

morton Street, then turn left on Throckmorton to pass in front of the President's Home and the white house just north of it.

A5

President's Home

The President's Home was completed in 1963 after the Old President's Home, located near the present All Faiths Chapel (C7), was destroyed by fire. President James Earl

President's Home (A5) *PS*

Rudder was the first occupant of the present house, which receives considerable use for social functions. The living quarters are located on the second floor.

The white house located north of the President's Home, at 100 Throckmorton, is currently the residence of the vice-president for student services. A small sign by its driveway lists its former residents.

Just beyond the vice-president's home, in a picnic area furnished by the Class of 1982, is a plaque recalling the many faculty and staff homes that have been moved from this area and other parts of campus.

Continue north on Throckmorton. In the small triangular esplanade to your right is the Spanish-American War Memorial.

First floor in President's Home (A5) *PS*

A6

Sanders Corps of Cadets Visitor Center

The area between Throckmorton and Coke streets, to your right, is Spence Park, the site of the Corps of Cadets Visitor Center, under construction in 1990 and 1991. The center will preserve and present the history of the Texas A&M Corps of Cadets in its Hall of Honor and assist in attracting high-quality students to the Corps and the university by providing a place where prospective students can meet with Corps administrators. The facility will provide offices for the Corps commander and key cadet staff members. An archives and library, an audio-visual gallery, and the Sanders Gun Collection (previously on display in the Memorial Student Center) will also be included in the center.

The center is named for Dr. Sam Houston Sanders (Class of 1922), a physician and educator who was honored as a Texas A&M Distinguished Alumnus in 1970.

At the north end of Spence Park, on Joe Routt Boulevard, is G. ("Pat") Foley's sculpture of A&M's Centennial Emblem, donated by the Class of 1976 on the university's hundredth anniversary.

Cross Joe Routt Boulevard—named for A&M All-American Joe Routt (Class of 1937), who died in the Battle of the Bulge in World War II—turn left, and proceed west to the entrance of the Rudder Tower and Theater Complex.

A7

Rudder Tower and Theater Complex

This twelve-story conference tower and theater complex

Rudder Tower and Theater Complex (A7) *PS*

was dedicated in memory of former Texas A&M President and Distinguished Alumnus James Earl Rudder (Class of 1932) on November 22, 1973. During the D-day assault in World War II, Rudder led the men of the 2nd Ranger Battalion up the hundred-foot cliffs at Pointe du Hoc, France, against heavy German resistance. Later in the war he commanded the 109th Infantry and won new honors in the Battle of the Bulge. The decorations and flags of his military career are on permanent display in the foyer of Rudder Auditorium.

After the war, Rudder served as mayor of Brady, Texas, and as commissioner of the General Land Office of Texas. As president of Texas A&M University from 1959 until his death on March 23, 1970, he initiated sweeping building programs and academic reforms on the campus. He

Flags and medals of Gen. James Earl Rudder (A7) *NP*

also served as president of the TAMU System from 1965 to 1970. It was under his administration, as Congressman Olin E. Teague explained at the dedication of this building, "that Texas A&M gained University status, doubled its enrollment, expanded its research programs, broadened its curriculum, upgraded academic and faculty standards, initiated a $100 million building program and, yes, even went co-ed."

Rudder Tower was built for multiple uses, providing facilities for both entertainment and continuing education. The tower is host to conferences with topics ranging from atomic energy to zoology. The ground floor of the tower houses the Campus Information Center, often described as Texas A&M University's window, where visitors can find maps and friendly directions on how to get "from here to there." In addition, the Information Center has viewer-controlled tape and slide presentations that blend descriptions of the university's traditions and ongoing educational programs. A multiple-projector production introduces visitors to the sights and sounds of Aggieland.

The third through the seventh floors contain comfortable conference rooms. Floors eight, nine, and ten house

Faculty Club, in Rudder Tower (A7) *PS*

the offices of the president of the university and the vice-president for finance and administration as well as the Placement and Athletic Department offices. The Faculty Club, on the top two floors, offers a spectacular view of the campus and surrounding countryside.

The east wing of the building houses the Theater Complex, which contains three performance areas: the Forum, with seating in-the-round for 250; the Theater, with seats for 750; and the Auditorium, with wide aisles and 2,500 seats. One of the Auditorium's unusual features is a special reverberation room that reduces extraneous sound. Through a system of pickups and delay circuitry, sound is transmitted from speakers in the auditorium to the listener's ear at the same time the unreverberated sound is received directly from the stage.

The Rudder Tower Exhibit Hall has 10,500 square feet of space for displays and exhibits. Art exhibits ranging from the works of El Greco and Piero di Cosimo to Frederic Remington and Charles M. Russell bring thousands of visitors to the center each year.

A plaque in the east wing recognizes Col. Richard J. Dunn, Texas A&M bandmaster from 1924 to 1946.

After exiting through the north doors of the Exhibit Hall onto Military Walk (C15), turn left and proceed west to Lamar Street.

A8

Simpson Drill Field

The open field located north of the Memorial Student Center across Lamar Street is the Drill Field, named in honor of Marine Lt. Gen. Ormond R. Simpson (Class of

Review on Simpson Drill Field (A8) *PS*

1936), an A&M Distinguished Alumnus who returned to
Texas A&M University, after retiring from military service,
and served as head of the School of Military Sciences until
his retirement from A&M in 1986. On this field the Corps
of Cadets holds its drills and reviews. The most impressive
is Final Review, when seniors participate in their last military review as members of the Corps of Cadets and turn
their commands over to next year's seniors.

Fifty-three live oak trees were planted around the field
in 1920 to honor the Aggies killed in World War I. Metal
plates attached to the trees name each student memorial-
ized and the battle in which he died. Some of the trees
have died, and thirty-five young trees have been added,
many in a second row on the north and east sides of the
field. A bronze plaque at the east end of the field tells the

story of the memorial trees. Another plaque beside the sidewalk on the same end of the field memorializes James E. Sarran, a sophomore student who was killed in 1955 when he saved the lives of two fellow students while working on the Aggie Bonfire.

Continue west along Lamar and enter the main (north) entrance to the Memorial Student Center.

A9

Memorial Student Center

The Memorial Student Center opened in 1950 and was formally dedicated on Aggie Muster Day, April 21, 1951, to former students who had died in World War II. The names of 916 of those Aggies are inscribed on bronze tablets at the main entrance.

Across the entryway is another plaque presented by a national organization in honor of 104 Aggies "who led and supported us during the gallant defense of Bataan and Corregidor from 8 December 1941 to 6 May 1942."

This building includes a cafeteria, a bookstore and shops, hotel facilities, a bowling alley, snack bars, meeting rooms, administrative offices, and lounge areas. It replaced the much older YMCA Building (C5) and the original Aggieland Inn (see C10) as a student gathering place. The second floor of the MSC contains large meeting and dining areas, the ever-expanding Student Programs office suite, a Student Finance Center that serves more than five hundred student organizations, and a browsing library. The Metzger Gun Collection on the third level contains many antique and exotic firearms.

Memorial Student Center (A9) *PS*

Selections from the university's permanent art collection hang in the Schiwetz Lounge adjacent to the main entrance. This area is named in honor of the first Texas State Artist, Distinguished Alumnus Edward M. ("Buck") Schiwetz (Class of 1921) and contains many examples of his art.

Across from the Schiwetz Lounge on the pillars of the north corridor hang portraits of Texas A&M's eight Medal of Honor winners. Proceed past the portraits to the east end of the corridor. To your immediate right is Room 104,

Metzger Gun Collection in MSC (A9) *PS*

the "Gallery," which houses scheduled temporary art exhibits. Turning right and continuing down the east hallway, you will pass the main student lounge (the "Flag Room) on the left; on the right are carved wood panels created for A&M's 1976 centennial celebrations by Professor of Architecture Rodney Hill and his wife Sue. The de-

Hand-carved wooden panels depicting A&M history (A9) *PS*

tailed carvings depict the first hundred years of Texas A&M's history. Just past the carved panels is the entrance to a snack bar.

Ahead of you is the MSC Gift Shop, and to your left and downstairs in the basement you will find the bookstore, the bowling alley, a brown-bag food area, and the head-

Flag Room lounge in the MSC (A9) *PS*

quarters of the world-famous Singing Cadets, the Century Singers, and other A&M singing groups.

An expansion of the Memorial Student Center begun early in 1990 will add some 160,000 square feet of floor space. A 20,000-square-foot visual arts display facility will extend the northeast corner of the MSC. A 90-foot expan-

Forsyth Galleries in the MSC (A9) *PS*

sion toward Rudder Tower will include an entirely new browsing library, additional meeting rooms, and an expansion of the Student Programs office. The MSC basement will be renovated and expanded with an entirely new food court, a television and video game area, an enlarged Singing Cadets practice facility, and relocated bowling lanes.

Along with the addition to the MSC, an L-shaped building also begun in early 1990 will wrap around the north and west sides of a 1,500-space parking garage across Joe Routt Boulevard from Rudder Tower. This building will house the Student Activities office, the Athletic Department, the Placement Center, and a new delicatessen/pastry shop.

Before leaving the MSC, return to the ground floor and proceed west along the south corridor past the etched glass windows of the MSC snack bar and cafeteria area. Turn left just past the post office. To your right are the MSC Forsyth Center Galleries (opened in 1989 in the former headquarters of the Association of Former Students). As you exit the south doors of the MSC and cross Joe Routt Boulevard, G. Rollie White Coliseum will be diagonally to your left.

A10

G. Rollie White Coliseum

"Jolly Rollie," or the "holler house on the Brazos," as it is variously known to students, was constructed primarily as a basketball arena (A&M has won six SWC titles since it was built) and is now also home court to the A&M volleyball team. The coliseum was completed in 1954 and dedicated to Brady, Texas, banker George Rollie White (Class of 1895), a member of the A&M Board of Directors from 1926 to 1955 and president of the board from 1945 to 1955.

The building doubles as the largest indoor assembly area on campus (maximum seating capacity 8,100) and is used for entertainment events and public ceremonies such as graduation and the annual Aggie Muster, held not only

G. Rollie White Coliseum (A10) *GJ*

on campus but at various locations throughout the world each April 21. The gymnasium floor was designed to be removable so that the facility could be used for stock shows, rodeos, or other events, but the floor has never been removed since the building was constructed. A number of additions made since 1954 include athletic ticket sales booths; offices; intramural handball, volleyball, and basketball courts; and exercise facilities.

After crossing Joe Routt, bear to your right and cross the small parking lot toward the Twelfth Man Statue (A11) and the north entrance to Kyle Field (A12).

Twelfth Man Statue (A11) *PS*

A11

Twelfth Man Foundation and Twelfth Man Statue

The small, one-story building between G. Rollie White Coliseum and DeWare Field House (A13) is headquarters for the Twelfth Man Foundation (formerly the Aggie Club), which raises funds for A&M athletic programs. Behind the building is G. ("Pat") Foley's statue *The Twelfth Man*, a gift of the Class of 1980. Plaques on the statue contain the words to Mrs. Ford Munnerlyn's song "The Twelfth Man" and a brief description of A&M's Twelfth Man legend.

The Twelfth Man is a unique Aggie tradition dating back to the Dixie Classic, a national championship football game against Centre College of Kentucky in Dallas on January 2, 1922. During the game, sophomore E. King Gill, a former reserve fullback, was in the press box serving as a spotter. As the rough game wore on and injuries took their toll, the Aggies were down to only one backfield substitute. Coach Dana X. Bible called Gill down to the playing field and asked him to suit up. Though Gill never got into the game, which A&M won 22–14, his willingness to serve started the tradition. Since that time Aggie coaches have called upon the spirit of the fabled Twelfth Man on many occasions. Aggies stand at football games to signify the students' readiness to enter the game, if needed–to be "the twelfth man on that fighting Aggie team."

A12

Kyle Field and Steed Conditioning Laboratory

The grounds for Kyle Field were reserved by the Board of Directors as a permanent athletic field on November 10, 1904. Edwin Jackson Kyle (Class of 1899), the professor of horticulture and dean of the College of Agriculture for whom the field was officially named by the board on April 28, 1956, was chairman of A&M's Athletic Council for many years following the turn of the century. Wooden bleachers were purchased by Kyle with his own money in

Kyle Field (A12), with SRO crowd of 78,000 *PS*

time for the first game played on the field, on October 7, 1905, and in 1907 Kyle purchased a covered stadium from the old Bryan fairgrounds.

The current stadium is the culmination of numerous addition and reconstruction projects. The first components of the present stadium were constructed in 1927. In 1929 the east stands and north end zone sections increased seating capacity to 35,000. A narrow upper deck and press box were added to the west stands in 1954. In 1967, a second deck was constructed over both east and west sides of the stadium. Because of burgeoning enrollments and heightened interest in football, in 1979 a third deck was added to both sides, along with new dressing rooms, a modern press box, and forty-eight luxury suites built between the second and third decks on the west side. The third deck raised seating capacity to 74,387, making the two-hundred-foot-high Kyle Field Stadium one of the largest and best-outfitted in the country. The East Kyle expansion, which includes classrooms, handball courts, and weight training rooms under the stands, was dedicated to Thomas Read in 1985. A Houston businessman, and not an alumnus of A&M, Read contributed heavily to scholarship funds in engineering and physical education.

In 1970 the natural grass playing surface was replaced with Astroturf. The "rug," as it is popularly known, has been replaced several times since then.

Dedicatory plaques in and just outside the north entrance to Kyle field recognize James Sullivan and Charles B. Moran. Sullivan was a member of the Feed Control Division and served as tennis coach during World War I and the 1920s and athletic council business manager until 1931. The plaque quotes Moran, "The Great Coach of the Texas Aggies, 1909–1914," as saying "I didn't come here to lose." Two other plaques recognize Edwin Jackson Kyle and the officers of the college, members of the athletic council, architects, and contractors.

Fifty-five American flags fly above the stands to honor the Texas Aggies who died in World War I. The two one-

Steed Conditioning Laboratory (A12) *GJ*

hundred-foot flagpoles located at the south end of the field were donated by Distinguished Alumnus John R. Blocker (Class of 1945) in memory of his brother, Lt. William B. Blocker, of the same class, who died in World War II.

A recent addition to the sports complex, dedicated in 1986, is the Netum A. Steed Conditioning Laboratory (at the southwest corner of Kyle Field), which provides one of the finest physical training facilities anywhere, with 40,000 pounds of free weights, an indoor forty-yard track, and an array of physiology research equipment. Steed (Class of 1942) was very active in the Association of Former Students and the Wichita Falls A&M Club. South of the Steed Building are the intramural tennis courts and varsity tennis courts, named in honor of Omar Smith (Class of 1937), longtime A&M tennis coach.

The graves of four Aggie mascots, all named Reveille, lie at the north end of Kyle field, "where they can always see the scoreboard." The first Reveille appeared on campus in the early 1930s. She got her name by vigorously protesting when the bugle call sounded for morning formation. She was named a general in the K-9 Corps, and her funeral in Kyle Field made international news. Next to the graves is an eternal flame, donated by the Class of 1983, which symbolizes the undying Aggie spirit.

From the north entrance to Kyle Field, return to Joe Routt Boulevard. You will pass the front of DeWare Field House on your left. When you reach the street, turn left and proceed west on Joe Routt past the entrance to Downs Natatorium and Cain Pool. By continuing west to the middle of the pedestrian bridge over Wellborn Road, you can have an excellent view of the West Campus and the athletic complex.

A13

DeWare Field House, Downs Natatorium, Cain Pool, and the West Side Athletic Complex

DeWare Field House was the original basketball gymnasium, built in 1924. Charles A. DeWare (Class of 1908), a three-year letterman in football, was paralyzed in his lower limbs after he left A&M, but he remained devoted to athletics and continued as an active Aggie supporter who

Wofford Cain Olympic Pool (A13) *GJ*

served as president of the Association of Former Students in 1921.

The P. L. Downs Natatorium, constructed in 1934, was named for P. L. ("Pinkie") Downs, a 1906 graduate who served on the A&M board from 1923 to 1932. Before he died in 1967, Pinkie served as "official greeter" for Texas A&M and raised maroon and white vegetables such as radishes and turnips at his home just south of the campus on Dexter Street. A widely circulated story tells how he once stopped at a funeral in Central Texas. When no one responded to the minister's call for a final word about the deceased, Pinkie reportedly said, "If nobody wishes to say

Olsen Field (A13) *GJ*

anything about the deceased, I'd like to say a few words about Texas A&M."

The Wofford Cain Olympic Swimming Pool, with eight fifty-meter lanes and a ten-meter diving platform, opened in 1962. It was named in honor of Distinguished Alumnus R. Wofford Cain, a 1913 graduate who served on the A&M board from 1969 to 1972.

Southwest of Kyle Field across Wellborn Road and the railroad tracks is more of the university's athletic complex, including the baseball stadium, named for Distinguished Alumnus C. E. ("Pat") Olsen (Class of 1923), who played for the New York Yankees with Babe Ruth and Lou Gehrig.

One of the finest college baseball stadiums in the nation, Olsen Field was dedicated in 1978, and the lighting was added in 1980. A crowd of 6,421 saw the Aggies hold the Houston Astros to a nine-inning, 1–1 tie in 1988 to set the stadium attendance record.

Just west of Olsen Field is the Frank G. Anderson Track and Field Complex, completed in 1986. This modern facility, which hosted its first SWC outdoor track and field meet in 1990, honors a former A&M Corps of Cadets commandant who coached track at A&M for twenty-five years. He produced two Olympic gold medalists, and his teams won nine Southwest Conference championships.

Adjacent to Olsen Field and the Anderson Track and Field Complex is the lighted W. L. Penberthy Intramural Field, dedicated to a former dean of men and head of the Physical Education Department, Walter Lawren Penberthy. More than 16,000 A&M students participate in competitive intramurals each year. In the middle of the intramural complex is the Lady Aggies Softball Field, home of the three-time national championship team.

From Wellborn Road, return eastward along Joe Routt and turn left on Clark Street. You will pass the Board of Regents' Annex (across Clark Street to your right), and Cain Athletic Hall will be to your left.

A14

Board of Regents' Annex

The A&M Board of Directors was renamed the Board of Regents of the Texas A&M University System in 1975, but the board remains organized according to a state law of 1913, which specifies that the board be made up of nine persons appointed by the governor of Texas to six-year terms.

The offices and conference rooms of the Board of Regents, as well as their quarters during their meetings and other visits to campus, are in this building attached to the hotel section of the Memorial Student Center and separated from the main building of the MSC by a small courtyard. The board moved to this headquarters in 1974 from the Old Board of Directors' Building, which once stood north of Sbisa Hall (see C14).

A15

Cain Athletic Hall

Cain Athletic Hall is a modern dormitory reserved for Texas A&M University athletes. Its "training table" dining facility is reputed to be one of the best in the nation. Like the Cain Swimming Pool (A13), the dormitory is named for R. Wofford Cain.

Texas Aggies played their first football game in 1896, defeating Ball High School of Galveston, 14–6. Texas A&M is a charter member of the Southwest Conference, which was organized in December, 1914.

Angling to your left (northwest) on Clark Street, you pass the Grove before arriving at Albritton Bell Tower.

A16

The Grove

The Grove dates from 1949–50, when it was built as a place for outdoor entertainment. Long used for yell practices, senior barbecues, and dances, it is now operated by a student committee of the Memorial Student Center. Summer evenings, movies are shown in the Grove for Aggies and their guests. On Parents Weekend in April, the Grove is the site of the annual Bevo Burn Bar-B-Q.

A17

Albritton Bell Tower

> I ring
> With pride and honor
> For all past, present and future
> Students of
> Texas A&M University.
>   – Inscription on Bell 4

The Albritton Tower is a gift to Texas A&M University from Martha and Ford D. Albritton (Class of 1943) and was dedicated on October 6, 1984. Albritton served on the Board of Regents from 1968 to 1975 and held many service positions with the university. He is a past president of the Association of Former Students and was recognized as a Distinguished Alumnus in 1977.

The tower is 138 feet tall and contains Westminster chimes, which ring every quarter hour. The forty-nine carillon bells, cast in France, can be played from a keyboard but are also programmed to play special seasonal music as well as the "Spirit of Aggieland." The three largest bells peal out in celebration of Aggie victories. The largest bell weighs 6,550 pounds, and the collection of bells totals seventeen tons. Each bell is cast with a relief of the seal of Texas A&M University. Twelve of the bells are inscribed

Albritton Bell Tower (A17) *PS*

Installation of the Ford D. Albritton, Jr., Bell *DG*

with names and dedicatory inscriptions, and twelve are inscribed with names of friends, former students, and administrators of the university. A time capsule in the bell tower is to be opened on Texas A&M's two-hundredth anniversary, in 2076.

Southeast of the tower on the corner of Simpson Drill Field is the monument commemorating Texas A&M's dead in World War I. Known as the West Gate Memorial, the monument was donated by the classes of 1923–26 and contains fifty-two names.

The Albritton Tower concludes Tour A and marks the beginning of Tour B (the West Campus) and Tour C (the Traditional Campus), which returns you to Rudder Tower.

View from the top of the Albritton Bell Tower (A17) at West Gate (B1),
looking east toward the Academic Building (C24) *PS*

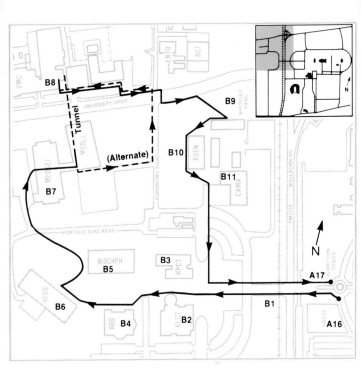

Tour B

THE WEST CAMPUS: START AND END AT ALBRITTON BELL TOWER (Distance: 1.5 miles)

From Albritton Bell Tower, walk westward and cross Wellborn Road (FM 2154) with the traffic lights at the corner of Old Main Drive. Be especially cautious while crossing Wellborn and the adjacent railroad tracks.

B1

West Gate

The intersection of Old Main Drive and Wellborn Road marks the old "West Gate" of the campus, the main entrance until the construction of State Highway 6 along the east side of campus in 1931. From the school's beginning until well into the 1930s, most students and visitors arrived on the campus by train. At first this point on the tracks was a flag stop for the Houston & Texas Central Railroad, but in 1883 the railroad built a permanent station near the West Gate which remained in use until 1958. The station was torn down in 1966. Passenger service resumed in 1989 when Amtrak and the City of College Station established a depot about a half mile south of here.

By 1877 students and residents had begun to mark out "Bryan" on school stationery and write in "College Station," though the City of College Station officially did not come into being until October, 1938. Faculty and staff lived on campus or commuted from Bryan by horse, train, or foot, or on an "interurban," which began service in 1910 but was displaced by the automobile in the 1920s.

The road leading west across the railroad tracks provides access to the Agricultural, Veterinary, and Medical complexes. Farther to the west is the Texas A&M Research Park, established in 1986.

Proceed westward toward the buildings of the Agricultural Complex.

Statue of Robert Justus Kleberg, Jr., Kleberg Center (B2) *PS*

B2

Kleberg Animal and Food Sciences Center

The more southerly of the two tall buildings ahead of you is the Kleberg Center. The equestrian statue on the south side of this building is that of Robert Justus Kleberg, Jr., who owned and directed the world-famous King Ranch from 1935 until his death in 1974. He was awarded

Atrium in the Kleberg Center (B2) *PS*

an honorary degree in agriculture from Texas A&M in 1941 for his contributions to Texas' cattle and livestock industries and for his support of Texas A&M. A bust of Kleberg stands in the center of the building's lobby. The building houses the College of Agriculture's Animal Science Department and features a greenhouse "solarium" interior. Cattle brands from every county in Texas decorate the stairwell walls in the northeast corner of the building.

"Twin towers" of the Heep Center (B3) *PS*

B3

Heep Center for Soil and Crop Sciences

The other "twin tower" of Texas agriculture on the West Campus is the Heep Center, located due north of the Kleberg Center. It was named for Minnie Belle and Herman F. Heep (Class of 1920). Herman Heep served on the A&M board from 1958 to 1961. This building's open, glass-roofed interior, with bridges on each floor between the two wings, creates one of the most interesting interior spaces on campus.

Texas A&M soil and crop scientists have contributed materially to the greater production of Texas farms. Improved strains of cotton, maize, peanuts, onions, and tomatoes are only a few of the truly significant developments in agriculture that have emerged from research programs of the Soil & Crop Sciences Department.

B4

Rosenthal Meat Science and Technology Center

Immediately west of the Kleberg Center is the Rosenthal Meat Science Center, completed in 1982 and named for Distinguished Alumnus E. M. ("Manny") Rosenthal (Class of 1942), chairman emeritus of Standard Meat Company. The Meat Science Center is perhaps best known to students and faculty at the university for its retail meat and dairy sales store. The ice cream available at the center is an Aggie "tradition" that the public is invited to share. Entry to the building is on the south side. On display in three trophy cases in the corridors of this combined office, laboratory, and classroom building are more than 380 awards

Walkways between wings of the Heep Center (B3) *PS*

and medals earned by student meat-judging teams over a period of fifty years. Another case contains a life-sized bronze bust of E. M. Rosenthal.

B5

Biochemistry/Biophysics Building

In addition to classrooms, the five-story Biochemistry/Biophysics Building, completed in 1989, has four modern teaching labs on the second floor. Upper floors contain

Biochemistry/Biophysics Building (B5) *NP*

computer facilities and thirty research lab suites for up to 240 faculty members and graduate students. These facilities include eleven cold rooms, six darkrooms, and three labs designed for containment of biological or potentially pathological materials. In addition, there is a large student lounge and a plant growth facility with light, humidity, air flow, and temperature carefully regulated. A specialized supply room contains biochemicals and liquid nitrogen for these labs and other facilities on campus.

A feature of the building is the "Ag CaFe" that can seat 220 people inside and another 75 on a covered patio. A two-week-cycle menu includes a salad bar, made-to-order pizza and other fast foods, and ice cream. Hours are 7:00 A.M. to 5:00 P.M., Monday through Friday.

Horticulture and Forest Science Building (B6) *NP*

B6

Horticulture and Forest Science Building

Another of the buildings in the Agricultural Complex with a solarium or atrium design, the Horticulture and Forest Science Building was completed in 1984. This build-

Solarium lobby of the Horticulture and Forest Science Building (B6) *PS*

ing is approximately one mile distant from classrooms on the far east side of campus. The lobby of the building has been designated the Benz Gallery of Floral Art in honor of Distinguished Alumnus M. ("Buddy") Benz (Class of 1932). Before his death, Benz arranged to have the internationally acclaimed Benz School of Floral Design, which he established in Houston in 1945, moved to Texas A&M. In addition, he gave a magnificent collection of floral art, which alternates in the lobby with various traveling exhibits. Also featured are four 350-year-old Chinese paintings and a woven thirty-foot by forty-foot wall hanging created by the Brazos Valley Spinners' and Weavers' Guild for the Texas Sesquicentennial in 1986.

The west mall sidewalk terminates at the Horticulture and Forest Science Building, and Tour B turns northward through the College of Medicine complex.

B7

Reynolds Medical Sciences Building and the Medical Sciences Library

The Texas legislature authorized establishment of a medical school at Texas A&M University in 1971. The first class of thirty-two students enrolled in the fall of 1977, and the first M.D. degrees were granted by the university in 1981. The first two years of medical training are completed on the A&M campus, while the last two years involve residency training in Temple at the Olin E. Teague Veterans' Center, the Scott and White Hospital and Clinic, or other approved hospital units. The medical program at Texas A&M is unique in that it seeks to produce an "undifferentiated physician," and students are required to receive experience with a medical unit or practitioner in a small town or rural area of Texas.

The Medical Sciences Building, completed in 1983, is named for Houston attorney Joe H. Reynolds, who served on the A&M Board of Regents from 1975 to 1989. Lecture halls are equipped for state-of-the-art telecommunications, including interactive, closed-circuit television transmitted via microwave over a dedicated television link with the college's clinical campus in Temple. The building also houses a permanent collection of seventy original works by local artists. Visitors may view the collection from 8:00 A.M. to 5:00 P.M., Monday through Friday.

Pedestrian tunnel under University Drive (FM-60) (B7) *NP*

The Medical Sciences Library (just east of the Reynolds Building) serves both the College of Medicine and the nearby College of Veterinary Medicine. The building, opened in 1985, also contains the Learning Resources Unit and the Biomedical Communications Unit of the College of Medicine. A collection of weavings, paintings, and sculpture by local artists is displayed in the library. A unique foam sculpture, *The War Within,* by John Walker, dominates the stairwell and is best viewed from the second floor. It depicts the confrontation between host and alien bodies in the bloodstream and suggests parallels with the weaponry fashioned by humans.

Directly north of the College of Medicine (across FM 60 or University Drive) is the Veterinary Medical Complex. A well-lighted basement-level tunnel beneath University Drive connects the two facilities and is accessible through a stairwell or elevator in the Medical Sciences Library lobby during normal business hours every day of the week and later on some weekdays. If you choose to cross University Drive at ground level, be extremely careful, and cross with the signal light at Agronomy Road (see alternate map route).

B8

Texas Veterinary Medical Center

The 1879–80 A. & M. College catalog listed D. Port Smythe, the college physician, as "Professor of Biology, Hygiene and Veterinary Science." A department of veterinary medicine was established in 1888, staffed and directed by Dr. Mark Francis, who has come to be known as the father of veterinary medicine in Texas. The School (now

Texas Veterinary Medical Center (B8) *PS*

College) of Veterinary Medicine was created in 1916 under the direction of Francis. Francis Hall (E17), located on the main campus near the Evans Library (E19), was completed in 1918 and was used for veterinary studies, as was the old Veterinary Hospital (now Civil Engineering, E5), until the first units of the present veterinary medical center were completed in 1954. The Clinical Sciences Building was added in 1981.

The Small Animal Clinic on the southwest corner of the complex and the Large Animal Clinic on the north side provide training for student veterinarians and services to the general public. Adjacent to the Small Animal Clinic is the main entrance to the Veterinary Hospital (where the pedestrian tunnel under University Drive exits), which contains a display on Veterinary College history, including photos of the graduating classes from 1920 to the present. East of that are the administrative offices of the College of Veterinary Medicine. A major interior renovation of the eastern wing was completed in 1987.

Agronomy Road, on the east side of the Veterinary Medical Complex, leads to the north past an array of veterinary, agricultural, research, and service facilities. These

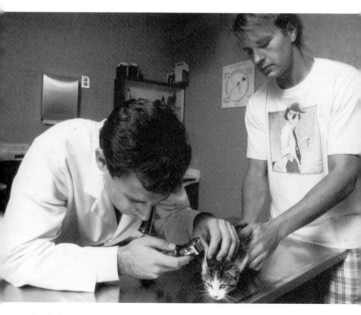

Small Animal Clinic (B8) *PS*

include the Veterinary Medicine Diagnostic Laboratory; the Entomology Research Laboratory and Biological Control Facility; the Forest Science, Cotton, and Agronomy laboratories; U.S. Department of Agriculture toxicology laboratories; and the university's administrative services units such as the Purchasing and Stores Building, Transportation Center, Commissary, and Physical Plant and Grounds Maintenance facilities.

Return to the south side of FM 60 at its intersection with Agronomy Road. Walk eastward toward the railroad overpass and then veer to the right into Eli Whiteley Park.

B9

Eli Whiteley Park

Eli Whiteley Park, containing a grove of pecan trees, is a small greenspace named in honor of Eli Lamar Whiteley (Class of 1941), who received the Medal of Honor for heroic service in World War II. Lieutenant Whiteley continued to lead his company in a desperate attack on strong German positions at Sigolsheim, Germany, in 1944, in spite of being wounded in the initial assault. When the war ended, Whiteley returned to his alma mater to pursue the peaceable profession of professor of agronomy until his death in 1986.

At Eli Whiteley Park, turn right and follow the narrow walk westward along the building wall and then around the front of the Agricultural Engineering Shops. For an alternate walk, continue through Eli Whiteley Park, then turn right and cross the parking lot behind the shops diagonally and walk south on the road along the railroad tracks.

B10

Agricultural Engineering Shops

In this group of buildings, sometimes referred to as the power and machinery laboratory or small engines laboratory, farm equipment such as plows, balers, and aircraft spray devices are invented, studied, and adapted for greater efficiency in agriculture.

Round the front of the main building of the Agricultural Engineering Shops and bear left through the parking lot of Cater-Mattil Hall.

B11

Cater-Mattil Hall

This building houses the Food Protein Center, which provides research and supporting instructional services for the curricula in Food Science and Technology, Food Engineering, and related disciplines. It is named for two professors who directed and sponsored significant research in cottonseed oil and soybean products. Dr. Carl M. Cater (Class of 1946) and Dr. Karl F. Mattil were pioneer researchers in the Oilseed Products Laboratory and the Food Protein Research and Development Center until their deaths in 1976 and 1977, respectively.

From Cater-Mattil Hall, return to your starting point at West Gate and Albritton Tower (A17), which is also the starting point for Tour C. Tour C will conclude at Rudder Tower (A7).

Large Animal Clinic (B8) *PS*

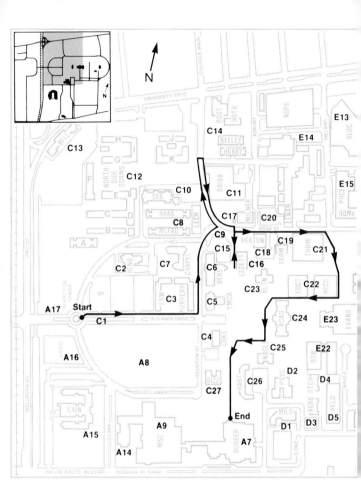

Tour C

C1

Old Main Drive

Stand under Albritton Bell Tower and look eastward
up Old Main Drive. For the first fifty years or so of Texas
A&M's existence, most students and visitors arrived at the
train stop across Wellborn Road (FM 2154) just south of
Old Main Drive. Imagine yourself walking into the campus a century ago when the drive was a dirt track on a bald,
treeless prairie. Imagine the campus without large oak trees,
paved streets, or wide sidewalks and with perhaps a half-
dozen buildings arrayed about the wood-frame Old Main
or, after 1914, the copper-domed Academic Building, and
you have a sense of the relative desolation and starkness
of the campus through much of A&M's early existence.

C2

Henderson Hall

Across the parking lot to your left as you walk east on
Old Main Drive is Henderson Hall, which served as the

Old Main Drive (C1) *PS*

university's athletic dormitory from 1961 until the completion of Cain Athletic Hall in 1974. After service for a time as a dormitory for women athletes, Henderson Hall became the headquarters of the Texas Engineering Extension Service. The building was named for an outstanding Aggie athlete, Robert William ("Jitterbug") Henderson

(Class of 1942), who won eleven varsity medals in five major sports (more than anyone else in A&M history) and was an All-American javelin thrower in track and field (1940–42). He served in the U.S. Army during World War II, and he won election to the Texas legislature in 1952 but was forced to resign because of poor health. He died of multiple sclerosis in 1955 at the age of thirty-six.

C3

Law and Puryear Halls

The next buildings on your left are Law and Puryear Halls, a pair of men's dormitories which began service in 1928. They are mirror-image buildings, constructed from the same plans, each containing 108 rooms. They have no ornamentation, and in some respects they mark the beginning of the era of efficiency in modern institutional architecture.

On this site a "tent city" was erected in 1906 to temporarily" house an overflow of students. As such things tend to happen, the wooden-floored tents continued to serve as student housing until World War I. At that time the tents were replaced by 165 sixteen-foot by sixteen-foot wooden shacks affectionately called "Hollywood" by the students. When rains came, they were called "Hollywood under the Sea."

One dormitory is named in honor of Francis Marion Law (Class of 1895), who served with great vigor and merit on the Board of Directors of the A. & M. College for twenty-seven years and was president of the board from 1924 to 1945. The other is named for Charles Puryear, who joined the A&M faculty in 1889 as an associate professor of engineering and physics. He became head of the Department of Mathematics and in 1907 was named the first "Dean of the College," a position somewhat equivalent to today's position of provost. He also was the first graduate school dean and served as acting president of the college on two occasions. Puryear had a very strong role in developing Texas A&M's modern academic programs.

C4

Coke Building

At the end of Old Main Drive, the first building diagonally to your right across the Houston Street intersection is the Richard Coke Building, completed in 1951. It houses some of the administrative offices of Texas A&M University, including the offices of provost and dean of faculties. Until 1989 it housed the offices of the president of the university.

The building was named on May 11, 1957, in honor of Gov. Richard Coke (1874–76), who dedicated the college on October 4, 1876. At the opening ceremonies Governor Coke announced: "The aim and mission of the Agricultural and Mechanical College of Texas, is, while preparing the young men of Texas for the high duties of American citizenship, at the same time to train their intelligence in the methods and appliances of science, and their hands for the skills which shall utilize them in the everyday pursuits of life. . . ."

The first president to occupy this building was Dr. Marion Thomas ("Tom") Harrington (Class of 1922), the first graduate of Texas A&M to serve in that position. This

Richard Coke Building (C4) *PS*

building was the first on the campus to have central air-conditioning. Students called it "Uncle Tom's Cabin."

After viewing the Coke Building, walk northward on Houston Street.

C5

YMCA Building

Across Houston Street from Puryear Hall stands the YMCA (Young Men's Christian Association) Building,

YMCA Building (C5) *PS*

completed in 1914 and financed by gifts from former students and from Mrs. John D. Rockefeller. The building served as the major student recreation center or "union" until the completion of the Memorial Student Center in 1950. Architects consider the YMCA a building of superior design and crafted detail. The building originally had two floor levels, but a third floor was added in the 1920s. The basement contained a bowling alley and a swimming pool, which has been boarded over for many years. A chapel, described in the thirty-ninth college catalog as "a charming piece of work," was lost by the installation of offices in the chapel lofts. Despite the changes, the building continues to be a highly functional structure which houses administrative offices and the Student Services office.

C6

Beutel Health Center

Just north of the YMCA Building is the Health Center, built in 1973 and named for Albert P. Beutel, a member of the Board of Regents from 1962 to 1974. The Health Center replaced the sorely outdated College Hospital built in 1916 to serve 700 students. History seems to repeat itself, for though the A. P. Beutel Health Center was designed to meet the needs of about 25,000 students, it now (with additions) serves about 40,000. This site was originally occupied by Mitchell Hall, which was built in 1912 and razed in 1972.

C7

All Faiths Chapel

The nondenominational chapel located across Houston Street from the A. P. Beutel Health Center is a gift of the

All Faiths Chapel (C7) *PS*

Interior of All Faiths Chapel (C7) *MB*

Association of Former Students. Completed in 1958, it has become a favorite place for Aggie weddings. Ernest Langford, who was a professor of architecture and archivist at Texas A&M, described the building as "beautiful and inspiring in its simplicity."

C8

Lechner, McFadden, and Haas Halls

North across Jones Street from the All Faiths Chapel are three residence halls constructed by the new modular system (developed by Distinguished Alumnus H. B. ["Pat"] Zachry [Class of 1922]) in which rooms or dormitory units are made of precast concrete and set in place by huge cranes. The newest dorm (facing the Fish Fountain) is a co-ed honors dormitory dedicated to Walter William Lechner (Class of 1914), one of the principal discovers of the north

McFadden Hall (C8) *PS*

portion of the giant East Texas oil field and a founder of the Texas Independent Producers Association. He served on the Texas Wildlife Commission for nine years. A $5-million gift from the Lechner family established the Lechner Scholarships, which benefit 130 high-achieving A&M students each year. The dorm along Jones Street is named for Ella C. McFadden of Fort Worth, who established a trust which endowed numerous undergraduate President's Scholarships and made other important contributions to Texas A&M. The third dorm in this group is dedicated to Distinguished Alumnus Richard E. Haas (Class of 1945), an oil operator and cattleman from Corpus Christi, and a benefactor of TAMU.

Fish Fountain (C9) *PS*

C9

Fish Fountain

Just past the All Faiths Chapel, Houston Street is bisected by a small park, near the center of which is the Fish Fountain, where Aggie Yell Leaders are dunked by freshman Corps members after an A&M football victory in Kyle Field. For a time during the 1970s Yell Leaders ended up in the Rudder Tower Fountain after a win. Fish Fountain was given by the Class of 1938 in memory of twelve classmates who made the supreme sacrifice in World War II. In 1975, the Class of 1977 paid to have the fountain renovated.

Pass the Fish Fountain and continue north on Houston Street.

C10

Special Services Building

Many "old Ags" will remember the Special Services Building, just west of the modular dorms, as the College Hospital. The building remained in service as a hospital from its opening in 1916 until the A. P. Beutel Health Center was completed in 1973. The building, incidentally, was noted as "the first hospital in the world to be equipped with showers throughout." The building currently houses the Department of Rural Sociology.

A plaque near the sidewalk along Houston Street east of the Special Services Building marks the site of the original Aggieland Inn, which was built in 1925 to serve campus visitors. The building was later used to house the

"Basic Division," which supervised and guided entering students from 1950 until the early 1960s. The Aggieland Inn was razed in 1966.

C11

Sbisa Dining Hall

Bernard Sbisa Hall is clearly one of the most important buildings on the A&M campus and has been in continuous use as a mess hall and restaurant since its completion in 1913. It was long reputed to have the "largest unobstructed dining room in the world (of slightly less than half an acre, 250 by 75 feet). Two additional dining rooms measure 80 by 110 feet, and 80 by 55 feet, respectively.

On the main floor, an efficient cafeteria/fast-food operation serves students. The Underground, a food court in the basement, provides a wide variety of culinary offerings. Bakery goods are available at Le Bun Shoppe and Mexican food at Tio Taco, while Mrs. Sbisa's Kitchen has hamburgers, fried chicken, and homemade soup and the Fortune Cookie provides oriental fare. Sandwiches are the specialty at Sbisa's Deli Section, a giant salad bar sells salads by the ounce, and you can finish off with an ice cream treat at the Sundae School. The Underground's hours are 10:30 A.M. to 7:30 P.M. during the week except Friday, when it closes at 1:30 P.M. It is closed Saturday, but open 4:00 to 8:00 P.M. Sunday. An adjacent study hall is open until 11:00 P.M. each day. Visitors are welcome. The Market, a large grocery and variety store at Sbisa, sells food as well as school supplies.

Bernard Sbisa was an Austrian-born New Orleans chef who joined the college staff in 1879 as steward and served

Sbisa Dining Hall (C11) *PS*

through 1926. Early on the morning of November 11, 1911, an older wooden mess hall near this site was destroyed by fire. It is said that in all his years, Sbisa was late with only one meal—the ten o'clock breakfast on the day of the fire.

Pass Sbisa Dining Hall and continue to the corner of Houston and Hogg streets.

C12

North Dorm Area

In the northwest corner of the main campus, to the west and north of the modular dorms (C8) and the Special Services Building (C10), are eleven residence halls built between 1930 and 1980 and named for the following people (with date of construction following in parentheses):

Dorm A   Rita Crocker Clements, wife of Gov. Bill Clements. (1980)

Dorm B   Lt. Thomas W. Fowler (Class of 1943), who received the Medal of Honor for gallantry in action in Italy on May 23, 1944. He was killed ten days later. (1965)

Dorm C   Army Sgt. George Dennis Keathley (Class of 1935), who was awarded the Medal of Honor for assuming command of his company in September, 1944, after all company officers were killed, and fighting on for fifteen minutes after being mortally wounded. (1965)

Dorm D   Air Force 2nd Lt. Lloyd D. Hughes (Class of 1943), who received the Medal of Honor posthumously for crash landing his aircraft and thereby saving most of the crew after the plane was damaged in a bombing mission in August, 1943. (1965)

Dorm E   Army Maj. Gen. Andrew Moses, commandant of cadets from 1907 to 1911. (1942)

Dorm F   Army Maj. Clarence R. Davis (Class of 1927) and Army Lt. Arthur E. Gary (Class of 1940), the first two A&M men killed in World War II. (1942)

Dorm G   Army Maj. Gen. George F. Moore (Class of 1908), commandant of cadets from 1938 to 1940, who was captured on Corregidor when it was surrendered

North Side residence hall room (C12) *PS*

in 1942. A legendary Aggie Muster was held on Corregidor only days before the surrender. (1942)

Dorm H   Army Pvt. Norman G. Crocker (Class of 1918), the first A&M man killed in World War I, when his ship was sunk by a German submarine in 1918. (1942)

Dorm I   Louis Lowry McInnis, a faculty member from 1877 to 1890 who served as chairman of the faculty (president) the last four years and as a member of the Board of Directors from 1905 to 1908. (1965)

Dorm J   Henry C. Schuhmacher (Class of 1892), a member of the Board of Directors from 1924 to 1940. (1965)

Dorm K   Thomas Otto Walton, former director of the Extension Service, who served as president of Texas A&M from 1925 to 1943. (1931)

C13

Bell Building

Northwest of the North Dormitory Area, at the intersection of University Drive and Wellborn Road, is the H. C. Bell Building. This large office building, the first ever built on campus oriented to true direction, was built in 1942. It faces due west. Referred to for many years as the U.S.D.A. Building because of the federal agriculture offices housed there, it was also known as the Triple-A Building in recognition of the Agricultural Adjustment Administration. Today it is occupied by the Texas A&M Research Foundation, the Public Policy Research Laboratory (which conducts the periodic Texas Poll), and other university offices. The building is named for Austin businessman H. C. ("Dulie") Bell (Class of 1939), a member of the Board of Regents from 1971 to 1982.

C14

Hobby, Neeley, and Hotard Halls

Across Hogg Street behind Sbisa Dining Hall are two modular residence halls, Hobby and Neeley Halls, which occupy the former site of the old Board of Directors' Residence, a two-story white frame building that had Southern-style verandas. The Directors' Residence, built in 1912, contained sleeping and dining rooms as well as a large conference room for the use of the college's directors when they gathered on campus. From 1974 until it was destroyed by fire in 1979, the building served as the home of the director of the newly established Texas A&M University Press, with the book publishing offices on the second floor.

Hobby and Neeley Halls were dedicated in October, 1983. Oveta Culp Hobby, who commanded the Women's Army Corps during World War II and served as the first secretary of the U.S. Department of Health, Education, and Welfare in 1953, is the widow of Gov. William P. Hobby and the mother of Lt. Gov. William P. Hobby, Jr. Marion J. Neeley (Class of 1922) is a Distinguished Alumnus and benefactor of Texas A&M.

Hotard Hall, once known as Dorm 13, is located just north of Hobby and Neeley Halls behind the U.S. Post Office at the North Gate of the campus. It was built in 1939 as living quarters for dining hall workers and served that purpose until after 1958, when the upper floors became student housing. Joseph Clifton Hotard became assistant food director in 1928 and then succeeded William Adam Duncan as director in 1937. He held the post until 1944.

From the corner of Houston and Hogg streets, retrace your steps southward on Houston and bear to the left as it curves into Ross Street. You will now be directly in front of the main entrance of Sbisa. At this point, turn right and walk a short distance along Military Walk, the paved esplanade that extends southward to Rudder Tower.

C15

Military Walk

Military Walk, which connected Sbisa Dining Hall and Guion Hall (which stood from 1918 to 1971 where the Rudder Tower and Theater Complex now stands), was closed as a street in 1971. This area was the central focus of campus life during the first part of the twentieth century. Other buildings once lining the walk included Austin Hall, Ross Hall, Foster Hall, Mitchell Hall, and the Assembly Hall. The class of 1936 dedicated the plaque located at the north entry to Military Walk in 1985.

C16

Legett Hall

Legett Hall and Milner Hall (C17) are built on the same plan. They originally contained 102 rooms and housed ap-

Legett Hall (C16) on Military Walk (C15) *PS*

proximately 200 men (and sometimes more). The dormitories were a new design, with each floor independent of the others and with no connecting stairways between floors. The idea was to provide privacy, quiet, and fire protection. When opened in 1911, Legett and Milner were the most modern dormitories on any campus, with four shower heads on each floor, "ample" toilet facilities, hot- and cold-water taps, and electricity for each student room.

Named for Judge K. K. Legett of Abilene, who served on the Board of Directors from 1901 to 1910 and was president of the board from 1905 to 1910, Legett Hall was completely renovated in 1979 for use as a women's residence hall.

The small park north of Legett Hall is the site of Gathright Hall, the second building constructed on the A&M campus. It was named for A&M's first president, Thomas S. Gathright. Completed in 1876, it remained in use until torn down in 1933. A bronze plaque next to one of the benches in the center of the park marks the location.

At this point, turn around and retrace your steps back to Ross Street, then turn right and proceed east past Milner Hall, Heaton Hall, Fermier Hall, and the Thompson Mechanical Engineering Shops.

C17

Milner Hall

Until undergoing substantial renovation to house the Mathematics Department in the mid-1970s, Milner Hall served as a men's dormitory, the purpose for which it was designed and constructed in 1911. Robert Teague Milner, for whom the building is named, was Texas Commissioner of Agriculture before accepting the position as president of the Agricultural and Mechanical College in 1908. He served as president until 1913, during a time of considerable growth and some controversy on campus. He also served on the A&M board from 1905 to 1908.

C18

Heaton Hall

Many Aggies bought their first books and supplies at the Exchange Store (or bookstore) that occupied this building beginning in 1925. It was renovated to serve as offices for the registration and admissions staff in 1977 and the next year was named for Homer Lloyd Heaton (Class of 1936), who served as registrar and dean of admissions from 1944 until 1972. One of Heaton's memorable experiences was being kidnapped by a student who was irate about the grades he had received.

C19

Fermier Hall

Emil Jerome Fermier joined the A&M faculty in 1906 as head of the Department of Mechanical Engineering and retired in 1927. Mechanical engineering professor Charles W. Crawford (Class of 1919), who wrote a history of the College of Engineering, recalled Fermier as one of the "most astute and smartest men" he ever worked with. Crawford noted that Fermier died only a few hours after

Fermier Hall (C19) *NP*

his wife passed away, in the fall of 1927. Fermier's Essex automobile failed to start when he headed for the telegraph office to tell his family of his wife's death, so he walked the eight blocks from the College Hospital (C10), climbed the steps to the operator's office, sat down and wrote, "Nora died tonight about eleven o'clock . . . ," and dropped dead. The board named the Mechanical Engineering Building for him in 1925, before his death, an unusual and distinctive honor for a faculty member.

The building was completed in 1920 and included a basement, three floors, and, at one time, an auditorium capable of seating three hundred students. Fermier Hall was substantially renovated in 1972.

C20

English Annex

This small, red brick building on the north side of Ross Street has lived a charmed life, so to speak. Built in 1923, it has been used variously by the Horticulture Department, the Radiological Safety Office (1958–76), the English Department (as a writing lab, from 1976 to 1981), the Mathematics Department (for graduate student offices), and, since 1986, by the Student Publications Office. Through it all, and in spite of minimal maintenance and renovation, the building has been saved from numerous attempts to demolish it.

C21

Thompson Mechanical Engineering Shops

Perhaps one of the best buys on campus was the structure referred to as the M.E. shops, on your right as you continue east on Ross Street. The shops contain over 45,000 square feet of work area and were built for about three dollars per square foot in 1922. The building continues to house tool rooms and classrooms, machine shops, carpentry shops, forge and foundry shops, and offices, all with good lighting and ventilation. In 1980 the shops were renovated and named for J. R. Thompson, president of Warren Electric in Houston, who was instrumental in the establishment of A&M's industrial distribution program.

After passing the Thompson Mechanical Engineering Shops, turn right into the fountain plaza area, completed in the late 1970s, that separates the shops on the right and the Chemistry Complex (E16) on the left. Turn right at the south end of the plaza and walk west.

C22

Harrington Education Center and Annex

The Harrington Education Center on your right, a classroom building with an adjoining office tower, houses many departments as well as the offices of the Colleges of Education and Liberal Arts. The center is named for Distinguished Alumnus Marion Thomas Harrington (Class of 1922), who began work as a chemist with Texaco in Port

Harrington Education Center and Annex (C22) *PS*

Arthur in 1922 and returned to accept a teaching position at Texas A&M in 1924. He became dean of the School of Arts and Sciences in 1948 and president of Texas A&M in 1950. In 1953 he became the second chancellor to head the Texas A&M System. He served in the dual capacities of president and chancellor from 1957 until James Earl Rudder became president in 1959. Harrington continued as chancellor until 1965 and retired from the university in 1971. Few administrators and faculty have had so positive an impact on the academic development of modern Texas A&M University. He died on May 14, 1990.

After passing the Harrington Center on its south side, continue past the Academic Building (C24) and then turn to your left. Before you turn, note Bolton Hall to your right.

C23

Bolton Hall

Known as the Electrical Engineering Building for many years, Bolton Hall was constructed in 1911 as the Electrical and Mechanical Engineering Building. It was called that until 1920, when the mechanical engineering program moved into Fermier Hall. On November 24, 1921, the first play-by-play radio broadcast of a football game was made from Bolton Hall. In 1989 the building was renovated and occupied by the Department of Political Science. In addition to classrooms, seminar rooms, and offices, it contains three computer laboratories and is wired to network all the computers with the university's mainframe computer.

Frank Cleveland ("Bear Tracks") Bolton joined the faculty in 1909 as the first head of the new Department of

Bolton Hall (C23) *PS*

Electrical Engineering. He became dean of engineering in 1922 and dean of the A. & M. College in 1931. He later served as acting president of Texas A&M in 1943–44 and then as president from 1948 to 1950. He retired from Texas A&M in 1955 after more than forty years of service.

C24

Academic Building

Construction on the Academic Building began in 1912, literally on the ashes of Old Main, the first building constructed at A&M, which had burned to the ground the previous year. The new building was designed by Samuel E. Gideon, at the time an instructor in architecture, and built

Academic Building (C24) *PS*

by Frederick Ernst Giesecke (Class of 1886), a professor of civil engineering who was designated "college architect" for that and many subsequent construction projects. The Academic Building was the second reinforced concrete building built on the campus (after Nagle Hall, next on this tour). It has the reputation among the university maintenance department personnel of being built like a fortress. Not only are the walls unusually thick, but Giesecke later confessed that because the idea of reinforced concrete was so new, he decided how much reinforcement steel was necessary and then doubled it.

The Academic Building is not only durable but also one of the most attractive buildings on campus. In its time the

Academic Building rotunda (C24) *PS*

Lawrence Sullivan Ross statue (C24) *PS*

building has housed presidential and personnel offices (including pay windows located at the west entrance), a bookstore, the library, academic offices, and classrooms. It continues to be one of the most heavily trafficked classroom buildings on the campus and houses the Faculty Senate offices and the University Honors Program.

The Liberty Bell replica, suspended at the second floor level under the rotunda, was given to the State of Texas in 1950 as part of a U.S. Savings Bond drive sponsored by private industry. Gov. Allan Shivers, in turn, presented it to Texas A&M in recognition of the sacrifices made by Aggies in the defense of the nation. Under the bell is a fourteen-foot-diameter mosaic of the university seal, the work of Joseph M. Hutchinson, an A&M professor of architecture. A gift of the Class of 1978, it originally contained 36,000 tiles. A giant service flag recognizing all Aggies who served and died in World War I hung in the rotunda of the Academic Building for a quarter of a century following its unveiling in Guion Hall in 1918. The flag is now preserved in the university's Archives (E23).

The statue of Lawrence Sullivan Ross (referred to as "Sully") outside the west entrance of the Academic Building was unveiled in 1919 to commemorate the man who was variously an Indian fighter, "boy captain" of Texas frontier forces, Confederate cavalry officer and brigadier general, sheriff, governor of Texas, and president of Texas A&M from 1890 until his death in 1898. The statue was sculpted by Pompeo Coppini, whose sculptures include numerous U.S. presidents and state heroes and the Alamo Heroes Cenotaph in San Antonio.

Periodically during the school year, Aggies gather on the lawn in front of the Academic Building to honor deceased students with Silver Taps. Under a dark sky, students and visitors stand quietly as the Ross Volunteer firing squad discharges a twenty-one gun salute. Six Aggie Band trumpeters sound the soulful notes from just below the Academic dome, and then everyone quietly withdraws.

Continue south past Sully's statue and you will be facing Nagle Hall.

C25

Nagle Hall

This building was the first reinforced concrete structure on the campus. Completed in 1909, it is now one of the two oldest buildings on campus (the other is the Analyti-

Nagle Hall (C25) *PS*

cal Services Building, D4). Constructed under the direction of Frederick Ernst Giesecke, it originally housed the Departments of Civil Engineering, Architectural Engineering, Drawing, and Physics.

James C. Nagle joined the faculty in 1890 as an associate professor of engineering and physics. He became the first dean of the College of Engineering when it was organized in 1911. The building has housed many academic departments and programs, including economics, geography, history, government, journalism, and, most recently, wildlife and fisheries sciences and recreation and parks. Recent renovation prepared the building for many more years of student and faculty use.

At Nagle Hall, turn right and proceed west toward Military Walk. Then turn left (south) to pass between Hart Hall and Bizzell Hall on your return to Rudder Tower.

C26

Hart Hall

The dormitory on your left is Hart Hall, erected in 1930 on the site of the old chapel (or Assembly Hall). Lacking the ornamentation of many of the early 1930s buildings, this dormitory was considered very efficient and progressive. It is named for L. J. Hart, a member of the Board of Directors from 1909 through 1924 and president of the board for six years. Along with Walton Hall (C12), Hart Hall was converted to use as married student housing for a time after World War II.

To your right as you pass Hart Hall is Bizzell Hall. The temporary parking lot north of Bizzell Hall is where Goodwin Hall stood from 1908 until 1989, the oldest building on the A&M campus at the time it was torn down. It was completed under a $50,000 legislative appropriation for a dormitory "to be known as Goodwin Hall." Naming a building in an appropriation bill is a most unusual gesture by the Texas legislature, which memorialized Charles Iverson Goodwin as "the author of the act accepting the land grant of the federal government and establishing the A. and M. College."

C27

Bizzell Hall

A dormitory from 1918 until the early 1960s, Bizzell Hall now contains administrative offices, including Planning and Institutional Analysis and the Office of University Research. Its west wing is the center of international programming for the campus. The building is named for William Bennett Bizzell, who served as president of the A. & M. College from 1915 to 1925, a time of rapid growth and development. Bizzell reprimanded Texans in 1923 for spending twice as much on tobacco as they spent on higher education. "Civilization costs something," he admonished. He left A&M to assume the presidency of the University of Oklahoma in 1925.

Tour C ends at the Rudder Tower (A7), which also marks the beginning of Tour D.

The Centennial Sculpture, "dedicated to a century of excellence," by George E. "Pat" Foley; the gift of the class of 1976, it stands on the south side of Joe Routt Boulevard between Throckmorton and Coke Streets *PS*

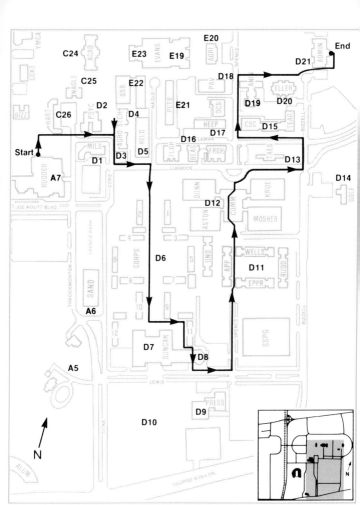

Tour D

Begin by walking eastward from Rudder Tower and Theater Complex (A7) and Hart Hall (C26). Continue ahead on the block-long section of Lamar Street. To your right will be the Military Sciences Building, and to your left, the Psychology Building.

D1

Military Sciences Building

This building, popularly called the "Trigon" by students because of its original three-sided shape and its connection with the military, was the Extension Service Building when it opened in 1924. An addition was built in 1961. The building now houses training programs for four branches of the service as well as the offices of the commandant of A&M's Corps of Cadets.

Texas A&M began as an all-male college with mandatory participation in the Corps of Cadets, which was organized along regular military lines and headed by a student officer corps. In 1916 the War Department established a Reserve Officers Training Corps (ROTC) program at Texas A&M. Students today may elect an advanced program lead-

Military Sciences Building or "Trigon" (D1) *JC*

ing to a commission in the Army, Air Force, Navy, Marines, or Coast Guard.

During World War I, Texas A&M sent a larger percentage of its total graduates into military service (49 percent) than did any other college or university in the United States. More than twenty thousand Texas Aggies served in World War II, and twenty-nine of them reached the rank of general; seven received the Medal of Honor.

Compulsory military training was abolished in September, 1965, and approximately ten years later the Corps of Cadets accepted its first female members. Today the Corps of Cadets enrolls only 5 percent of the total student population, but it remains an important and distinctive element in student leadership, school spirit, and pride.

Across Lamar Street, to your left as you pass the Military Sciences Building, is the Psychology Building (formerly the Physics Building).

D2

Psychology Building

Built for the Physics Department in 1920, this structure is unique in that it was used for its original purpose for sixty-seven years. Additions to the building were made in 1951, again in 1961, and most recently in 1987, when it was renovated for use by the Psychology Department. The 58,000-square-foot building contains five research laboratories and audio and video labs.

Immediately ahead, across the "elbow" formed by Lamar Street and Coke Street, is the Eugene Butler Building, and on its north side stands the Analytical Services Building.

D3

Butler Building

This building was constructed in 1918 and housed the Feed Control Service, which funded its construction. It served as administrative headquarters for the Texas Agricultural Experiment Station until those offices were moved to the System Administration Building in 1951. The Texas Agricultural Experiment Station was authorized by the twentieth Texas legislature under the provisions of the Hatch Act (1886) and was organized on the A&M campus in 1888. The first director of the Agricultural Experiment

Station was Dr. Mark Francis, who is sometimes referred to as the "father of the Texas cattle industry" because of his successful work on the control of Texas fever (tick fever). Since that time the Texas Agricultural Experiment Station has contributed enormously to the welfare of the state through its research on crops and livestock. For a number of years this building was known as the Agronomy Building. In 1988 it was named for Eugene Butler, retired editor-in-chief of *Progressive Farmer* magazine.

Butler Building (D3) *JC*

D4

Analytical Services Building

Built to serve as headquarters for the Texas Agricultural Experiment Station in 1909, this building is one of the two oldest on campus (Nagle Hall being the other). Its two stories and basement have housed portions of the Colleges of Agriculture, Education, and Science. It contains a classroom, laboratories, and offices.

Turn right (south) on Coke Street and then left (east) on Lubbock Street. The modern building on the corner of Nagle and Lubbock is Heldenfels Hall.

D5

Heldenfels Hall

This laboratory and classroom building, built in 1979, was named for Distinguished Alumnus H. C. ("Tony") Heldenfels (Class of 1935), of Corpus Christi, Texas, a member of the Board of Regents from 1961 through 1974 who served as president of the board from 1965 to 1967. Heldenfels Hall has two large lecture rooms seating 308 each and five lecture rooms which can handle more than 100 students each. There are ten physics labs, in which demonstrations can be conducted to dramatically illustrate various principles of physics. There are eleven biology labs on the third floor, and in the hall are fossil and skull displays and a backlighted transparency display. Twelve chemistry labs occupy the fourth floor, and in the basement, entered from the south stairwell, is the Learning Resources

Center, which features audio tutorial equipment and a modest computer lab.

Turn to your right at the Nagle Street intersection and proceed south across Lubbock Street to the Corps Plaza.

D6

Corps Dorm Area

The memorial by the arches leading into the Corps Dorm Area (also known as "the Quad" or "Twelve Area) honors those Texas Aggies who died in the service of their country since World War II, including many Korean and

Entrance to Corps of Cadets quadrangle (D6) *PS*

Vietnam War dead. This memorial, originally established in front of Duncan Dining Hall in 1969 with more than 325 names, was moved to its present location on Aggie Muster Day, April 21, 1987. More names were added at that time and again in 1989, bringing the total to 383.

After the Corps of Cadets became voluntary in 1965, the dormitories in this area were reserved for Corps members, but space is also assigned to "civilian" students when rooms are available. The dormitories were built in the late years of the Great Depression, and architects and administrators were directed to build facilities that would provide the maximum number of rooms at the lowest possible cost. The result was a spartan, military-style facility generally devoid of amenities. Since then, the dorms have been made more comfortable with the installation of air-conditioning, carpeting, paneled ceilings, and modular furniture. Student lounge buildings were constructed adjacent to them in the late 1960s.

The first building inside the arches on your right, Kiest Hall, will continue as the headquarters for the Corps of Cadets until completion of the Sanders Corps of Cadets Visitor Center (A6) in 1992. The small museum located in the Cadet Guard Room of Kiest will also be moved to the new building.

The twelve dormitories were completed in 1939 and are named for the following individuals:

Dorm 1   David Wendell Spence, professor of civil engineering, 1892–1917, and dean of engineering, 1913–17.

Dorm 2   Edwin J. Kiest, editor and publisher of the *Dallas Times-Herald* and member of the Board of Directors, 1927–45.

Dorm 3   Robert W. Briggs (Class of 1917) of Pharr, member of the Board of Directors, 1937–45.

Corps Plaza memorial to post-WWII Aggie war dead (D6) *JC*

Dorm 4   Charles P. Fountain, professor and head of the Department of English, 1904–21.

Dorm 5   Charles S. Gainer (Class of 1890) of Bryan, state representative, 1914–18; state senator, 1928–32.

Dorm 6   Walter G. Lacy (Class of 1895), president of the Citizens National Bank of Waco and member of the Board of Directors, 1924–41; board vice-president 1934–41.

Dorm 7   Turney W. Leonard (Class of 1942), winner of the Medal of Honor for heroic leadership against two superior enemy divisions in 1944 at Kommerscheidt, Germany.

Dorm 8   William George Harrell (Class of 1943), recipient of the Medal of Honor for continuing to fight during the invasion of Iwo Jima on March 3, 1945, in spite of a broken thigh and the loss of both hands.

Dorm 9   Eli Lamar Whiteley (Class of 1941), winner of the Medal of Honor in action at Sigolsheim, Germany, on December 27, 1944. (See Eli Whiteley Park, B9).

Dorm 10   Byrd E. White, member of the Board of Directors, 1922–35.

Dorm 11   Henry Hill Harrington, professor of chemistry, 1887–1908, and president of A. & M. College, 1905–1908. (This dorm is also known as the "Home of the Fightin' Texas Aggie Band.")

Dorm 12   Joseph Utay (Class of 1908), member of the Board of Directors, 1935–41.

Dorms 7, 8, and 9 were originally named for Henry C. Schuhmacher (Class of 1892), Louis Lowry McInnis (Class of 1895), and George Rollie White (Class of 1895). In 1954 the new coliseum (A10) was named for White, and in 1969 new dormitories in the North Dorm Area (C12) were named for Schuhmacher and McInnis.

Bugle Stand in front of Duncan Dining Hall (D7) *PS*

The bugle stand, with its megaphone for amplifying the bugle calls, located near Duncan Dining Hall, once stood inside the traffic circle at Old Main Drive and Houston Street, adjacent to the YMCA Building. The stand was funded by the Class of 1936 and is dedicated to the memory of classmate Edward O'Brien Bellinger.

D7

Duncan Dining Hall

At the south end of the Quad is the Corps of Cadets dining hall, completed in 1939 and named for William

Adam Duncan, the supervisor of subsistence from 1920 to 1937. Duncan and Bernard Sbisa (see C11), were responsible for feeding Texas Aggies for sixty years. In 1988 the university renovated the dining hall to include multiple cafeteria serving lines, specialty counters, and fast foods.

This building, incidentally, is constructed on the site of the old campus cemetery, which was moved to a location south and west of the campus (near the intersection of Luther Street and Marion Pugh Drive).

Walking east and around the corner of Duncan Dining Hall will take you to the E. V. Adams Band Hall.

Adams Band Hall (D8) *PS*

D8

Adams Band Hall

The "Fightin' Texas Aggie Band," famous for its precision marching at football games, was organized in 1894 with 13 members. Joseph F. Holick and Arthur N. Jenkins were local residents who organized the band, and Holick served as bandmaster for many years. By the 1930s the band, under the leadership of Col. Richard J. Dunn (1924–46), numbered some 100 students, but after World War II it grew rapidly. It included some 267 members in 1968, and it exceeded 300 by 1971.

The band hall, constructed in 1970, is named for Col. Edward V. Adams (Class of 1929), director of the band from 1946 until 1973.

The elevated corridor between Adams Band Hall and Duncan Dining Hall leads to Lewis Street and a view of the John H. Lindsey Building, home of Texas A&M University Press, and the nearby site of the fabled Aggie Bonfire.

D9

Lindsey Building

The building directly ahead of you across Lewis Street houses the Texas A&M University Press, which publishes scholarly and general-interest books (such as this guide), on subjects ranging from Texas history and art to military history and agriculture. John H. Lindsey (Class of 1944), past president of the Association of Former Students and a Texas A&M Distinguished Alumnus, was instrumental, along with A&M President and Chancellor Jack Kenny Williams, in bringing Frank H. Wardlaw to the campus to establish the press in 1974. Wardlaw had previously organized and headed the university presses at the University of South Carolina and the University of Texas.

After the old Board of Directors' Residence (see C14), first headquarters for the press, burned in 1979, the press was housed in trailers until the new building was ready. The Frank H. Wardlaw Collection of Western Art housed in this building may be viewed during regular working hours Monday through Friday.

Lindsey Building (Texas A&M University Press) (D9) *JC*

D10

Aggie Bonfire (Duncan Field)

If you take this tour during late October or in November, you can observe some of the activity surrounding con-

Texas Aggie Bonfire (D10) *PS*

struction of the Aggie Bonfire on the field behind Duncan Dining Hall, to the west of the Lindsey Building.

Students have signaled the annual gridiron contest between Texas A&M and the University of Texas with a pregame bonfire since soon after the turn of the century. The bonfire began on the main drill field (A8) as a pile of debris burned the night before the game in 1909. In the 1930s the pile had grown to enormous proportions, and in 1935 students decided that the fire required more than the usual flammable refuse, so they appropriated numerous outhouses and a farmer's log barn for fuel. The farmer complained bitterly, and thereafter the bonfire came under the supervision of the Commandant of Cadets and college administrators. In 1955 the bonfire was moved from the drill field to its present site.

The bonfire is now a massive engineering feat requiring thousands of students, heavy equipment, and untold hours of labor. The stack of tons of logs, sometimes towering over sixty-five feet (A&M set the world bonfire record of 107 feet, 10 inches in 1969), is ignited on that special night each year to signify the Aggies' determination to "beat the hell outta t.u." and their undying flame of love for Texas A&M. The only year the bonfire was not ignited was 1963, when it was dismantled because of the assassination of U.S. president John F. Kennedy.

From the Adams Band Hall, proceed east on Lewis Street and turn left (or north) on Spence Street, which ends in a pedestrian mall. To your right is the new two-thousand-car Southside Parking Garage, and to your left is the Col. Joe T. Haney Drill Field, named for the former student (Class of 1948) who directed the Aggie Band from 1973 to 1989. Just ahead are five modular dormitories built in 1981 and 1989.

D11

Modular Dormitories

The first dormitory to your right is named for Manor rancher George Eppright (Class of 1926), who gave the university property adjacent to the Austin city limits worth more than $16 million. Another land gift from Eppright endowed two chairs at the university and funds scholarships for the Corps of Cadets.

On your left is a dorm named for Distinguished Alumnus Leslie L. Appelt (Class of 1941), longtime trustee of the Texas A&M Development Foundation and past president of the Association of Former Students. This successful Houston real estate developer was instrumental in establishing the Visitor Information Center in Rudder Tower (A7) and assisted in creation of A&M's Center for Education and Research in Free Enterprise. Parallel to and just west of Appelt Hall is the dorm dedicated to Ammon Underwood (Class of 1907) in 1981. Underwood gave Texas A&M a one-million-dollar piece of real estate at Buchanan Dam in central Texas, endowed four A&M President's Scholarships, and willed his estate to the university.

At your far right, along Bizzell Street, is a dorm named for Margaret Rudder, widow of A&M President James Earl Rudder and a longtime supporter of A&M. The next dorm to your right is named for Clyde H. Wells (Class of 1938), a twenty-four-year member of the A&M Board of Regents. He was chairman of the board from 1969 to 1981, president of the Library Development Council, and a councilor for the A&M Research Foundation.

Continue north to the Commons, the focal point of another major dormitory complex. A passage beneath the hall-

ways on either side of the Commons leads to its front area on the north, or you may enter the Commons through the double doors on the loading dock.

D12

The Commons

Construction of the Commons, a central dining and lounge area for two dormitories for women and two for men, signaled the "new look" of the A&M campus at the beginning of the 1970s. Krueger and Mosher Halls, the two buildings connected to the Commons on the east side,

C. C. ("Polly") Krueger Hall (D12) *PS*

were the first two dormitories on the campus constructed for women students. Although a few women attended classes as "unofficial" students as early as the 1870s, and others received special permission to enroll in the 1920s and 1930s, Texas A&M University remained an all-male institution into the 1960s. Only in 1971 did the university catalog observe that Texas A&M was a "coeducational university admitting all qualified men and women to all academic studies. . . ." Today, undergraduate male and female enrollments are often equal, with women outnumbering men in entering classes. C. C. ("Polly") Krueger (Class of 1912) was founding president of the San Antonio A&M Club, served as president of the Association of Former Students, and was on the A&M board from 1947 to 1953. Edward J. Mosher (Class of 1928) chaired the executive committee of Mosher Steel Company.

Companion dormitories on the west side of the Commons are Dunn and Aston Halls. J. Harold Dunn (Class of 1925) headed Shamrock Oil and Gas Corporation and chaired the Century Council that outlined goals for A&M's centennial year of 1976. He served on the A&M Board of Regents from 1953 to 1959 and was board vice president the last two years. James W. Aston (Class of 1933) was chairman of the board of Republic Corporation. All of these men have been recognized with Texas A&M's Distinguished Alumnus Award.

The Commons has a cafeteria that seats three thousand people, the Common Denominator snack bar, and a mini-market with groceries and school supplies.

Pass around or through the Commons to its north entrance, then turn right on Lubbock Street and continue eastward to Bizzell Street.

Albritton Bell Tower (A17) *PS*

Bonfire (D10) *PS*

Lawrence Sullivan Ross statue (C24) *PS*

Reveille *PS*

(*Above*) System Administration Building (D21) *PS*
(*Below*) Review (A8) *PS*

(*Above*) Academic Building (C24) *PS*
(*Below*) System Administration Building (D21) *PS*

(*Above*) Flag Room of the MSC (A9) *PS*
(*Below*) Academic Building (C24) *PS*

Aggie gridders *PS*

D13

Texas Agricultural Experiment Station Annex

To your left, the Texas Agricultural Experiment Station Annex, across Lubbock Street from Krueger Hall, is an interesting building because it was built for horses, not people. Originally constructed in 1932 as a stable for fifty horses, it was converted into an information center for the Texas Agricultural Experiment Station in 1953. It later housed the Department of Recreation and Parks for a time, and it then became the Forest Science Building until that

Texas Agricultural Experiment Station Annex (D13) *TA*

Weather vane atop Agricultural Experiment Station Annex (D13) *PS*

department was moved to the West Campus in 1984. It is currently used for various administrative offices of the Experiment Station. Two weather vanes located atop the "horse barn" are examples of early Texas folk art and have a special (and inexplicable) mystique for many Texas Aggies.

At the corner of Bizzell and Lubbock, look diagonally to your right to see the university's golf course.

D14

Golf Course and Clubhouse

The university's eighteen-hole golf course is spread across the southeast corner of the campus. The development of the course began as an effort of the Student Life Committee, which contributed $4,000 for planning and construction in 1948. The Association of Former Students then pledged an additional $25,000, and construction began in January, 1950. The clubhouse and extensive course remodeling, which included a modern irrigation system, were added in 1972.

Turn left at Bizzell Street, walk a short block, then turn left again on Lamar, passing the front of the Agricultural Experiment Station Annex on your left.

D15

Teague Research Center and Computing Services Complex

Across Lamar Street from the "horse barn" (D13) is the Olin E. Teague Research Center and Computing Services Complex (formerly called the Data Processing Center). The Teague Center houses the Graduate College as well as technical support offices for engineering and computer sciences. The Computing Services Complex houses the university's mainframe and support computer hardware and is in many ways the nerve center of the university and its research components.

Olin E. ("Tiger") Teague (Class of 1932), born in Woodward, Oklahoma, received eleven decorations for bravery

Olin E. Teague Research Center (D15) *PS*

in World War II, including the Silver Star, the Bronze Star, the Croix de Guerre with Palm, and the Purple Heart. He won election to Congress in 1946, and during his long tenure there he served on the Veterans Affairs Committee and then the Committee on Science and Astronautics, where he made important contributions to the developing American space program. He was named a Distinguished Alumnus in 1966.

After passing the Teague Center, pause at the corner of Lamar and Spence streets and look ahead and to the south side of Lamar to see a row of three brick buildings with greenhouses in the rear.

D16

Beasley Laboratory and Greenhouses

The nearest of the row of one-story brick buildings with greenhouses, at the corner of Lamar Street and Spence, is the Forest Genetics Greenhouse and Laboratory. At the farthest end, at the corner of Lamar and Nagle, is the Floriculture Building and Greenhouse. Between them, in the middle of the block, is Beasley Laboratory, named for James O. Beasley (Class of 1932), an A&M researcher and pioneer in the field of cotton genetics who was killed in Italy during World War II. The Beasley Lab contains plant science offices and laboratories.

Turn right on Spence Street and proceed north.

Interior of the Beasley Laboratory and greenhouses (D16) *PS*

D17

Herman F. Heep Building

The building on the northwest corner of Spence and Lamar, not to be confused with the Heep Center for Soil and Crop Sciences on the West Campus (B3), is also dedicated to former regent Herman F. Heep. It was originally known as the Dairy Sciences Building. It is now home for some offices of the Department of Wildlife and Fisheries Science and has offices, classrooms, and laboratories for the departments of Agricultural Economics, Chemistry, and Veterinary Medicine. The smaller building behind it, facing Spence Street, is the Old Creamery Building, where the products of A&M dairy herds were once processed and made available to the public. That milk, cheese, and ice cream is now sold at the Rosenthal Meat Science and Technology Center on the West Campus (see B4).

Continue north along Spence until you arrive at the corner of a large grassy mall on the right. The building on your left, on the west side of Spence, is the Pavilion, and the building on your right, facing the mall, is the Animal Industries Building.

D18

The Pavilion

Originally the Stock Judging Pavilion or Animal Pavilion and now simply the Pavilion, this structure, built in 1917, until the mid-1980s contained a dirt-floored arena that could seat approximately twenty-five hundred people. It was used for livestock demonstration and show training.

The Pavilion (D18) *PS*

Renovation in recent years included flooring of the central livestock arena, addition of a second floor, and conversion of the spectator stands to offices. The building now houses registration, student financial aid, and student activities offices. The snack bar and information offices in the building are open to the public.

Turn right and continue along the south side of the mall in front of the Animal Industries Building.

D19

Animal Industries Building

The mall on the north side of the Animal Industries Building was the "agricultural quadrangle" of the 1930s

Animal Industries Building (D19) *PS*

campus. The Animal Industries Building, one of the major features of that quadrangle, was dedicated to "Pioneer Livestock Men of Texas" in 1936. U.S. senator Tom Connally made the dedicatory address, and U.S. congressman Richard M. Kleberg accepted on behalf of the people of Texas.

This building, which houses the Range Science Department and extensive meats laboratories, is one of the most decorated structures on campus; a multitude of animal heads and skulls, ears of corn, sheaves of grain, and cornucopias adorn the exterior. The ironwork on the doors features cattle brands from throughout the state.

Campus tradition holds that a ghost haunts the building—the ghost of a meat laboratory manager who accidentally cut his femoral artery and bled to death in the lab. The story, still circulating on the campus, is that the old custodian of the building, Henry Turner, used to leave the elevator on the lower floor at night so that the ghost would have easier access to it. When the elevator was not left in its proper position, it was said, unusual events could be expected or apparatus would disappear.

Exterior detail on the Animal Industries Building (D19) *TA*

Eller Building (D20) *NP*

D20

Eller Building

The fifteen-story Oceanography and Meteorology Building was completed in 1972, and in 1988 it was named in honor of David G. Eller (Class of 1959), chairman of the A&M Board of Regents from 1983 to 1989. The Department of Oceanography was authorized by the Board of Directors in 1949 as a precursor of Texas A&M's maritime academy in Galveston (now Texas A&M University at Galveston). Texas A&M University was one of the first four universities to be designated a federal Sea Grant college in 1966. The university now operates its own naval fleet from the Galveston port, including a number of smaller research vessels and a 473-foot combination passenger/freight training vessel—the *Texas Clipper*—launched in 1944.

The Eller Building, tallest on campus, also houses the dean's office and other departments of the College of Geosciences, including the Department of Meteorology, with its own weather observation laboratory on the top floor. Tours of this facility must be arranged in advance. A cartographic (map-making) unit in the building supplements the college's work with maps such as the ones in this book.

D21

System Administration Building

The System Administration Building is important not just because it has housed the offices of chancellor of the Texas A&M University System but also because its construction in 1932 symbolically marked the beginning of what might be termed the modern age of Texas A&M. Af-

System Administration Building (D21) *PS*

ter facing the railroad on the west, and in some respects the past, for many years, Texas A&M turned to face the automobile age, represented by the new highway on the east, and the future.

The building was designed in a thoroughly classical mode by Professor C. S. P. Vosper and was built by the indefatigable college architect, Frederick Ernst Giesecke. Interior walls, the main stairway, pilasters, ceilings, and floors of the building are treated in meticulous detail. Offices are large, the lobby ceiling is fifty-three feet high, and, as longtime archivist Ernest Langford concluded, the building is "the most grandiosely conceived structure ever erected on the campus."

The architect worked idealized portraits of A&M students into the capitals of the fourteen Ionic columns across the front, and considering that the structure was built when Texas A&M was an all-male military school, he was somewhat prescient in including one portrait of a young woman, Sarah Orth (Mrs. James W. Aston of Dallas), the daughter of William A. Orth, who was superintendent of construction on the building.

Heavy bronze doors bearing ornate A&M emblems and stylized Greek figures are backed by multicolored glass panels. Above the front doors are cast stones depicting Stephen F. Austin, the father of Texas, and Mirabeau B. Lamar, the father of Texas education. A map of Texas, in terrazzo tile and brass, depicting the history of Texas through the days of the Republic is worked into the floor in the main lobby; inadvertently (or intentionally?), Aus-

Decorated capital on column, System Administration Building (D21) *TA*

Greek figures on doors, System Administration Building (D21) *PS*

Gilded friezes, System Administration Building (D21) *PS*

tin was placed on the wrong side of the Colorado River.

The flagpole in front of the building stands on a five-sided pedestal that rests on a five-pointed star base. It was donated by the Class of 1934 shortly after the building was completed. The class repaired and rededicated it in 1979. Relief panels at the base feature robed Greek figures and a cadet wearing the insignia of a field artillery captain. Other panels list that era's administration and faculty members and the A&M presidents from 1876 to 1934.

The System Administration Building marks the conclusion of Tour D and the beginning of Tour E, which ends at Rudder Tower (A7).

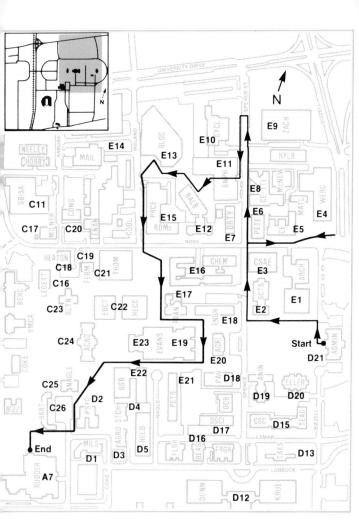

Tour E

OLD MEETS NEW: SYSTEM ADMINISTRATION BUILDING TO RUDDER TOWER (Distance: 1.5 miles)

From the System Administration Building, begin Tour E by walking toward Spence Street along the north side of the grassy mall.

E1

Langford Architecture Center

The Architecture Center is actually a complex of three buildings, one completed in 1962 and the others in 1978. This facility contains a changing showcase of works by students and faculty members. A new visualization laboratory, located just to the right as you enter from the mall, contains work stations that link sophisticated computers and display terminals to simulate environments, buildings, and urban developments. Atop the smaller building in the rear, a unique sky simulator laboratory, with a twenty-eight-foot-diameter dome, enables students and researchers to study light patterns, shadows, window shading, and passive solar heating concepts by making it possible to duplicate clear and overcast sky conditions.

The center is dedicated to Ernest Langford (Class of 1913), professor of architecture, head of the Department

(*Above*) Langford Architecture Center (E1) *CA*
(*Below*) Visualization laboratory, Langford Architecture Center (E1) *CA*

of Architecture (1929–57), and university archivist (1957–70). During his tenure as department head, A&M awarded 782 degrees in architecture, and Langford counted all his students as *his* boys, in a fashion analogous to the older, paternal relationship of institution to student. Langford participated in the organization of the City of College Station in 1938 and served twenty-four years as its mayor.

A small Serum Laboratory, built in 1917, occupied this site until the 1970s. From 1937 until 1965 it was used as a museum, and for many years it contained an Egyptian mummy that is now on permanent loan to the Houston Museum of Natural Science.

E2

Scoates Hall

This Agricultural Engineering Building, located west of the Langford Architecture Building and facing the grassy mall, is named for Daniel Scoates, professor and head of the Department of Agricultural Engineering (1919–39). The building was completed in 1932 (the same year the System Administration Building, Geology Building, and many others were completed). Scoates Hall features ceramic tile facings, an ornate stone belt course on the windowsill line of the third floor, and cast stone agricultural symbols, farm implements and scenes, goat heads, and cornices with owl figures. Intricate ironwork frames the entrance and was used to construct the lightpost there. Laboratory space in the rear lower level was designed for the study of gasoline engines, tractors, and farm machinery. Today the building is a general office and classroom building.

Turn right after passing Scoates Hall and proceed north

Intricate iron grillwork, Scoates Hall (E2) *TA*

to Ross Street. *You will pass between the Computer Science and Aerospace Research Building on your right and the newest wings of the Chemistry Complex (E16) on your left.*

E3

Aerospace Engineering and Computer Science Building

The Computer Science Department occupies three floors of this eight-story building, completed in 1989. Eight

Aerospace Engineering and Computer Science Building (E3) *PS*

labs are used to teach freshman courses in graphics, artificial intelligence, and real-time systems. Seven labs provide state-of-the-art facilities for software research and development, cognitive systems visualization, computer design of architecture, discrete computation, robotics, and real-time systems. The computer science program was initially established as part of the Department of Industrial Engineering and became an independent department within the College of Engineering in 1982.

The facilities of this building include special laboratories with water and wind tunnels for the study of aerodynamics and fluid dynamics; high-speed, stereo-imaging cameras and computers for motion analysis; a fully operational and instrumented jet engine; and computer work stations set up for computer-aided design and engineering.

Turn right at Ross Street and walk to the corner of Ross and Bizzell to view the Wisenbaker Engineering and Research Center.

E4

Wisenbaker Engineering and Research Center

Completed in 1983, the Engineering and Research Center represented a major and greatly needed addition to the College of Engineering, which had become one of the largest in the nation. The building houses the offices of the dean and vice-chancellor for engineering, the Texas Engineering Experiment Station, and various institutes and agencies operating under the authority of the College of Engineering. Laboratories, including the Materials and Construction Industry Laboratory, are located on the lower level of the building, and offices and conference rooms are located on the upper two levels. The building is named for A&M Regent Royce E. Wisenbaker (Class of 1939) of Tyler, who served as president of the Association of Former Students in 1966 and was recognized as a Distinguished Alumnus in 1973. He is considered the father of Texas A&M's President's Endowed Scholarship Program and was instrumental in creating the Association of Former Students Century Club program.

Reverse your path and move west on Ross Street to the corner of Ross and Spence. The first building you pass on your right is the Civil Engineering Building.

E5

Civil Engineering Building

The Civil Engineering Building opened for service in 1932 as the Veterinary Hospital, which explains the animal heads and figures decorating the stone exterior. In 1954 Civil Engineering moved from Nagle Hall to the larger quarters in the former Veterinary Hospital. The undergraduate civil engineering program is now headquartered here. Smaller buildings in the middle of this block include the Concrete Materials Laboratory; the McNew Engineering Laboratory, named for John Thomas Lamar McNew (Class of 1918), who headed the Civil Engineering Department in the 1940s and who initiated plans that resulted in the incorporation of the City of College Station in 1938; and the Hydromechanics Laboratory. The Hydromechanics Lab and the Concrete Materials Lab were once horse barns used in conjunction with the old Veterinary Hospital.

Civil Engineering Building (E5) *PS*

E6

Richardson Building

At the corner of Ross and Spence, the ten-story Joe C. Richardson, Jr., Petroleum Engineering Building, completed in 1989, features research laboratories for drilling operations, reservoir management, production operations, and enhanced oil recovery. Inside, a vertical opening from the roof to a twenty-five-foot-deep casing set in the basement floor permits accurate simulation of oil well recovery operations. An imaging center, moved from the Wisenbaker Building, where it was put into operation in 1988, contains computer-aided tomography and magnetic resonance scanning devices for the study of drilling core samples. Joe C. Richardson (Class of 1949), an independent oil and gas operator from Amarillo, served on the Board of Regents from 1981 to 1987 and was named a Distinguished Alumnus in 1989.

Turn right on Spence Street and proceed north through the area of the campus devoted mainly to engineering education. Across Spence from the Richardson Building is the W. T. Doherty Building.

Richardson Building (E6) *JC*

Demonstration oil well behind Doherty Building (E7) *JC*

E7

Doherty Building

The W. T. Doherty petroleum engineering building was completed in 1960. The building is of contemporary design, and its exterior is of buff-colored brick with blue porcelain-enameled aluminum (rather than the traditional tile) panels. Oilman W. T. Doherty (Class of 1922) was a member of A&M's Board of Directors from 1953 to 1959 and board president from 1955 to 1959. He was named a Distinguished Alumnus in 1966.

Behind the Doherty Building, on Ross Street, is a variable-speed demonstration well with a five-hundred-foot shaft that reaches a water formation. Fluid measurements from the well are taken on computer monitors inside the Doherty Building.

E8

Civil Engineering/Texas Transportation Institute Building

This 1987 addition to the College of Engineering complex houses the headquarters and graduate program of the Civil Engineering Department and the Texas Transportation Institute. Engineering Design Graphics occupies two floors of the adjacent CE/TTI Lab Building, with four drafting labs that accommodate a thousand students each semester and three computer graphics labs that have 110 individual computer stations.

In June, 1950, the Texas Transportation Institute was established to do research for the state's highway department. It is now the largest university-based research organization in the United States, conducting research in all forms of transportation. Safe lighting for streets and

Civil Engineering/Texas Transportation Institute Building (E8) *PS*

highways, development of roadside safety features through crash testing, development of new materials and designs for highway pavements and structures, and the planning and design of new urban mobility systems are a few of the more visible areas in which TTI researchers are working. In addition, they conduct studies in transportation economics, policy, planning, and accident analysis.

At "Pie Are Square," on the ground floor of this building, you can obtain breakfast, sandwiches, hamburgers, and other fast foods. It is open from 7:00 A.M. to 5:00 P.M., Monday through Friday.

The CE/TTI building is connected to the Wisenbaker Center and the McNew Engineering Laboratories by second-story skywalks.

E9

Zachry Engineering Center

This four-story building contains more than seven acres of floor space and houses many offices for departments of the College of Engineering. The interior includes an open lobby illuminated by a "sawtooth" skylight, balconies, and auditorium and lecture hall complexes. A teaching nuclear reactor and small particle accelerator are located in the building.

The Engineering Center was named in honor of Henry B. ("Pat") Zachry (Class of 1922) in 1972. The internationally recognized construction contractor from San Antonio became a member of A&M's Board of Directors in 1955 and served through 1961, including two years as president of the board. He was a great benefactor of Texas A&M

Interior, Zachry Engineering Center (E9) *NP*

University and received Distinguished Alumnus status in 1964.

At the Zachry Engineering Center, cross Spence Street toward the Cyclotron Building, then turn south along Spence to the Engineering/Physics Building.

E10

Cyclotron

A cyclotron strips nuclear particles from atoms and accelerates them to high velocity for research in chemistry, physics, biology, engineering, and medicine. A&M's cyclotron began operation in 1967, and recent modifications have made it one of three superconducting cyclotrons in the world. The Cyclotron Institute, organized in 1963 as an independent agency, conducts basic research, on the properties of the atomic nucleus, for example, and develops cyclotron-related techniques for application to nonnuclear problems. From the mid-1970s to the early 1980s, the Cyclotron Institute, in cooperation with Houston's M. D. Anderson Hospital and Cancer Institute, pioneered in the treatment of certain types of cancer with neutron bombardment.

E11

Engineering/Physics Building

Completed in 1986, the Engineering/Physics Building houses laboratories, offices, and classrooms for the Department of Physics and offices for engineering faculty. It is

Engineering/Physics Building (E11), with glass-enclosed "skywalk" *PS*

noted for its modernistic skywalk, which connects upper floors of separate wings.

The south wing contains offices, while the north wing has classrooms and research labs. Physics labs have trenches under the floors for various pieces of equipment, liquid nitrogen delivery systems, and a major helium liquefaction facility. Concrete pads on springs shield experiments from outside vibrations, and special rooms isolate electromagnetic radiation experiments.

Classrooms occupy the second floor, and mechanical engineering labs are on the third and fourth floors. In an energy systems lab, air-conditioning systems, heat pumps, and heat exchangers are studied, and the rotor dynamics lab tests high-speed bearings. The Design Institute devises new types of test apparatus for use in the labs. Three wind tunnels are used to study the efficiency of automobile bodies, telephone and light poles, and aircraft wings. The building also has a large machine shop, said to be the best on campus.

Turn west under this building's skywalk and continue across a plaza to the new wing of the Halbouty Geosciences Building.

E12

Halbouty Geosciences Building

Michel T. Halbouty (Class of 1930), a Distinguished Alumnus and prominent Texas consulting geologist and oilman, is appropriately associated with the Geosciences Building, which was formerly known as the Geology-Petroleum Engineering Building. Completed in 1932, the

Halbouty Geosciences Building (E12) *JC*

building, according to architect Ernest Langford, "beggars all descriptions." The older four-story portion of the building is in the shape of a capital **T**, and until 1972 it had a central tower that was inconsistent with and disproportionate to the remainder of the building. But in this architectural madness there was reason: the tower structure concealed a large water tank that maintained equal pressure in the hot water lines of the campus heating system. The south entrance, facing Ross Street, features castings of seashells, pebble mosaics, and recessed doors with iron grillwork. A heroic panel over the side entrance symbolizes petroleum exploration.

The new north wing of the Halbouty Geosciences Building was completed in 1985.

South entrance to Halbouty Geosciences Building (E12) *TA*

The plaza area between the Engineering/Physics Building and the Halbouty Building leads in a northwesterly direction to the John R. Blocker Building.

E13

Blocker Building

Construction of the John R. Blocker Building began in 1979, and many energy-saving features were included in its design. It is also the only recent campus building oriented on a true east-west axis. When it was completed in 1981 it was the largest building on campus in terms of floor space. The building houses the Texas Real Estate Research Center, the College of Business Administration and the departments of English and Theatre Arts as well as other components of the College of Liberal Arts. The Academic Computer Center located in this building features labs containing minicomputers and more than two hundred microcomputers. Distinguished Alumnus John R. Blocker (Class of 1945) was a member of the Board of Regents from 1977 through 1983. He and his wife Jeanne funded a chair in finance and business with a $1 million endowment.

Continue on past the Blocker Building to Ireland Street. Across Ireland are the Northside Parking Garage and the university's extensive maintenance facilities and power plant.

E14

Northside Parking Garage and Power Plant Area

This two-thousand-space parking garage on the west side of Ireland Street was completed in 1988 to give some relief

Interior, Blocker Building (E13) *PS*

to strained parking conditions on campus that resulted from increased enrollment in the late 1980s.

The area adjacent to the parking garage contains the A&M System Facilities and Planning Office, a power plant, cooling towers, a water tower, warehouses, and campus mail facilities.

Now turn south on Ireland Street and proceed to the corner of Ireland and Ross. The Printing Center and the Reed McDonald Building will be to your left. For light refreshment, there is also a snack bar with vending machines on that corner.

E15

Printing Center and Reed McDonald Building

The Printing Center (formerly called the Press Building) was constructed in 1955, and a wing was added in 1960. The A&M student newspaper, the *Battalion,* is printed here, as are the university's bulletins, booklets, and numerous brochures and mailing pieces. Complete photographic studios and processing facilities are located in this building. Connected to the Printing Center on the corner of Ross and Ireland streets stands the Reed McDonald Building, named for the longtime director of the Feed and Fertilizer Control Service. It has distinctive red bands of aggregate stone. Construction was financed mainly from the fees charged for testing the contents of commercial feeds and fertilizers and tagging the bags. This agency now operates as part of the Texas state chemist's office, headquartered here. A&M's Office of Public Information; Agricultural Communications; and the Journalism Department, including the *Battalion*'s editorial offices, are also in the building.

Reed McDonald Building (E15) *PS*

Cross Ross Street and proceed south through the fountain mall. The Chemistry Complex is to your left.

E16

Chemistry Complex

The oldest of the three buildings in the complex was built in 1929. It is adjoined on the east by two wings, the southern one completed in 1981 and a newer and larger addition along Ross Street completed in 1988. Today the

Ornate castings, entrance to original Chemistry Building (E16) *TA*

Newest wing of the Chemistry Complex (E16) *PS*

complex is one of the finest chemistry laboratory, classroom, and office facilities in the nation. The structures provide an interesting contrast in architectural styles, with the oldest building, designed by C. S. P. Vosper, seeming to cling to a classical decorative motif while the new buildings use clean, efficient lines with brick and glass. The elaborate ornamentation in the 1929 building appears to be stuck on, in a way foreshadowing the clean lines of modern construction but clearly denoting the affection for a more ostentatious past.

In the original Chemistry Building, Vosper employed elaborate color schemes using tile, paint, and terrazzo and somewhat affected designs that included classical geometric patterns, animal heads, the human face, skulls, bones, and fossils. The inscription to the left as you approach the main entrance (near the front corner of the building) is from Aristotle: "Let us first understand the facts, and then we may see the cause." On the right side is a quotation from J. Von Liebig: "The secret of all who make discoveries is to look upon nothing as impossible."

After passing the old Chemistry Building, continue south-ward and turn left at the end of the mall. As you walk east, Francis Hall and the old Engineering Building are on your left.

E17

Francis Hall

One faculty member-administrator who had an enormous influence upon the development of the modern university, particularly its programs in veterinary medicine, was Professor Mark Francis. Francis joined the faculty in 1888 as professor of veterinary science and veterinarian of the Texas Agricultural Experiment Station and continued as professor and dean of the College of Veterinary Medicine until his death in 1936.

Francis Hall was completed in 1918 and was used for veterinary studies, as was the old Veterinary Hospital (E5), until the first units of the present Texas Veterinary Medical Center (B8) were completed in 1954. The building contains a large lecture room/amphitheater that was once used for surgical demonstrations. From 1954 to 1981 the building was home for the College of Business Administration, and it is now used by the Recreation and Parks Department.

Francis Hall (E17) *PS*

E18

Engineering Building

This rather plain building, constructed in 1952, originally contained the offices of the dean of engineering, the

Engineering Building (E18) *PS*

Aerospace Engineering Department, Architecture Research, and Industrial Engineering. Engineering Design Graphics was in the building from 1958 to 1988. Ultimately, the building will house only Anthropology and Nautical Archaeology, although a portion of the College of Architecture occupies the first two floors while a fourth floor is added to one of the architecture buildings.

In front of the Engineering Building, turn right and proceed south between the Sterling C. Evans Library (E19) and the Agriculture Building (E20) toward the Pavilion (D18).

E19

Evans Library

At the center of the main campus lies the Sterling C. Evans Library, the academic heart of Texas A&M University. The library complex houses the university Archives and Special Collections in addition to nearly two million volumes. Computers and laser disks provide rapid access to books and information, both on the premises and in bibliographic holdings and collections across the country.

The large, modern building you see is the result of numerous additions and renovations. The oldest part of the structure is the Cushing Library (now the Archives), located on the west end across a mall area from the Academic Building. You will see it as you pass the south side of the library a little later in this tour. In 1967 the Cushing Building had become inadequate, and an addition at that time enlarged the library nearly eightfold. The five-year-old Texas Engineers' Library was enveloped by the main building during this remodeling. Evidence of the older structure includes the dedication plaque on the first floor of the main library and curious sunken student lounges on the second floor. The new structure included carrels for private study and seminar rooms. Prophetically, Dr. James P. Dyke, then director of the libraries, observed that, given the growth rate of the university, an expansion of equal size might be needed in the near future.

In 1973 the Library Complex was named for Sterling C. Evans (Class of 1921), former head of the Federal Land Bank in Houston, first president of the Houston Bank for Cooperatives, and later general agent of the Farm Credit Bank of Houston. Evans, named a Distinguished Alum-

Sterling C. Evans Library (E19) *TA*

nus in 1973, served two terms on the Texas A&M Board of Regents and was president of the board in 1963–64 and 1964–65. He is a major supporter of the Texas A&M University Library and was the first chairman of the Friends of the Library.

To meet the needs of the growing faculty and student body in 1977 the university began the six-story addition at the east end of the complex. During this project the older parts of the facility were completely remodeled and modernized.

The interior of the library is well worth the time it takes to explore and browse. The C. C. ("Polly) Krueger Collection of fine oil paintings hangs throughout the building along with other objects of art. In addition, there are always displays highlighting some aspect of the library's collections.

E20

Agriculture Building

Directly across from the main entrance to the library is the Agriculture Building, completed in 1922. It is a four-story classroom and office building which housed the dean of the College of Agriculture for about ten years. It was

Agriculture Building (E20) *TA*

envisioned as part of a "splendid quadrangle," with agriculture on the east, the Academic Building on the west, the Stock Judging Pavilion on the south, and Francis Hall and other projected buildings on the north, with open space in the area where the library now stands. The building is now the home of the Agricultural Economics Department.

Turn right at the Pavilion (D18) and walk westward along the south side of the library. Heading toward the Academic Building (C24), you pass the Peterson Horticulture Building and the Biological Sciences Building, on your left.

E21

Peterson Building

The Peterson Horticulture Building was constructed in 1962 and originally called the Plant Sciences Building. Many of the programs once housed here have been transferred to the new agricultural complex on the West Campus. The building included twenty-three laboratory rooms, six regular classrooms, a large lecture room, and faculty offices. It was named in 1985 for Distinguished Alumnus L. F. Peterson (Class of 1936), who endowed a faculty chair in petroleum engineering. This Fort Worth independent oil operator served on the A&M Board of Regents from 1963 to 1975 and was board president two of those years. The building is used by the Plant Pathology and Microbiology Department and the Soil and Crop Sciences Department. It is also home to the English Language Institute, which ensures that foreign students are proficient in English before they enroll at Texas A&M.

E22

Biological Sciences Building

Construction on the east wing of this building began in 1950, and the west addition was completed a little more than a decade later. The latter employs post and beam construction and more glass and brick facing, but both designs were based on economy and efficiency. Both the Biology and Plant Sciences departments, which originally occupied the Peterson and Biological Sciences buildings, have been relocated, and both buildings are now in use as general classroom and office buildings.

Biological Sciences Building (E22) *PS*

E23

Cushing Library Wing

Before you turn left to round the corner of the Biological Sciences Building, pause and look to the right at the Cushing Library Wing, the oldest part of the Sterling C. Evans Library Complex, which faces the mall behind the Academic Building. This building was named for Col. E. B. Cushing, chairman of the Texas A&M Board of Directors from 1912 to 1914. It was completed in 1930.

Cushing Library Wing (E23) *TA*

The exterior of the Cushing Library is neoclassical in style and decorated with Texas motifs such as steer's skulls and rams' heads on the capitals. Doorway decorations combine an ancient architectural theme with southwestern plants. Between the pilasters are names selected by a committee of deans to represent the greatest minds in the fields of human endeavor: Austrian botanist Gregor Mendel, founder of genetics; German botanist Julius von Sachs, founder of plant physiology; English essayist and reformer Francis Bacon; U.S. architect Charles Bulfinch; English scientist Michael Faraday, who worked with electricity and magnetism; Scottish physicist James Clerk Maxwell; French chemist and bacteriologist Louis Pasteur; English poet and dramatist William Shakespeare; Greek philosopher Plato; Scottish steam engine developer James Watt; English mathematician and natural philosopher Isaac Newton; and first U.S. president George Washington.

Our footsteps now lead in a southwesterly direction to the Rudder Tower. The buildings encountered along the way are described in earlier pages, but may be reviewed as follows: Academic Building (C24), Nagle Hall (C25), the Psychology Building (D2), the Military Sciences Building (D1), Hart Hall (C26), and finally the Rudder Tower (A7).

Afterword

We hope that this guide has been clear in its directions and informative about the campus features you have seen along the way. If you have any suggestions or corrections that might improve this book, please write to "Guided Tour," Texas A&M University Press, Drawer C, College Station, Texas 77843-4354, and your comments will be considered for the next edition.

Index

A&M clubs, 4

A&M College Rings, Josh Sterns Collection of, 4

Academic Building, 59, 82–88, 155, 158, 160, 161

Academic Computing Center, 146

Adams, Col. Edward V., 103–104

Adams Band Hall, 103–104, 107

Aerospace Engineering, Dept. of, 154

Aerospace Engineering and Computer Science Building, 131–32

Ag CaFe, 48

Aggie Club, 26

Aggieland Inn, 18, 69–70

Aggie Muster, 18, 24, 73, 99

Aggie spirit, 31

Agricultural Adjustment Administration, 74

Agricultural and Mechanical College of Texas, 62, 78

Agricultural Communications, Dept. of, 148

Agricultural Economics, Dept. of, 116, 158

Agricultural Engineering, Dept. of, 129

Agricultural Engineering Building, 129

Agricultural Engineering Shops, 55–56

Agriculture, College of, 8, 27, 97, 157

Agriculture, U.S. Dept. of, 55

Agriculture Building, 154, 157–58

Agronomy Building, 96

Agronomy Laboratory, 55

Albritton, Ford D., 36

Albritton, Martha, 36

Albritton Bell Tower, 3, 35, 36–38, 41, 56, 59

All Faiths Chapel, 9, 65, 67, 69

Alumni Association, 3

Analytical Services Building, 88, 97

Anderson, Frank G., 34

Anderson Track & Field Complex, 34

Animal Industries Building, 116–19

Animal Pavilion, 116

Animal Science, Dept. of, 43

Anthropology, Dept. of, 154

Appelt, Leslie L., 108

Architectural Engineering, Dept. of, 89

Architecture, College of, 154

Architecture, Dept. of, 127–29

Architecture Center, 127–29

Architecture Research, 154

Archives, 87, 155

Aristotle, 152

Armillary Sphere, 8

Arts and Sciences, School of, 82

Assembly Hall, 76, 89

Association of Ex-Cadets, 3

Association of Former Students, 3, 4, 8, 24, 31, 32–36, 66
Aston, James W., 110
Aston, Mrs. James W., 123
Aston Hall, 110
Athletic Dept., 16, 24
athletic dormitory, 34–35, 60
Austin, Stephen F., 123
Austin Hall, 76

Bacon, Francis, 161
Bagley Hall, 7
Ball High School, 35
Band, Aggie, 104, 107
baseball stadium, 33
Bataan, Philippines, 18
Battalion, The, 148
Battle of the Bulge, 12, 13
Beasley, James O., 115
Beasley Laboratory, 115
Bell, H. C. ("Dulie"), 74
Bell Building, 74
Bellinger, Edward O'Brien, 102
Bellinger Bugle Stand, 102
Benz, M. ("Buddy"), 50
Benz Gallery of Floral Art, 50
Benz School of Floral Design, 50
Beutel, Albert P., 65
Beutel Health Center, 65, 69
Bevo Burn Bar-B-Q, 36
Bible, Dana X., 27
Biochemistry/Biophysics Building, 47
Biological Control Facility, 55
Biological Sciences Building, 159, 160
Biology, Dept. of, 159
Bizzell, William Bennett, 90
Bizzell Hall, 89–90
Blocker, Jeanne, 146
Blocker, John R., 30, 146
Blocker, Lt. William B., 30
Blocker Building, 146

Board of Directors, 34, 74. *See also individual names*
Board of Directors' Residence (old), 74, 105
Board of Regents' Annex, 34
Bolton, Frank Cleveland ("Bear Tracks"), 82
Bolton Hall, 7, 82–83
Bonfire, 18, 104, 106–107
bowling lanes, 23
Bracewell, Searcy, 8
Brady, Texas, 13, 24
Brazos Valley Spinners' and Weavers' Guild, 50
Briggs, Robert W., 99
Bronze Star, 114
Bryan, 41–42
Bulfinch, Charles, 161
Business Administration, College of, 146, 152
Butler, Eugene, 95–96
Butler Building, 95–96

Cadet Guard Room, 99
Cain, R. Wofford, 33, 35
Cain Athletic Hall, 34, 35, 60
Cain Pool, 31, 35
Campus Information Center, 14, 15
carillon bells, 36
Cartographic Services Unit, 121
Cater, Dr. Carl M., 56
Cater-Mattil Hall, 56
cemetery, old campus, 103
Centennial Emblem (sculpture), 12
Centennial Wood Carvings, 20
Centre College, 27
Century Club, 133
Century Council, 110
Century Singers, 20
Chemistry, Dept. of, 116
Chemistry complex, 81, 149–52

Citizens National Bank of Waco, 101
Civil Engineering, Dept. of, 53, 89, 133, 137
Civil Engineering Building, 133
Civil Engineering/Texas Transportation Institute (CE/TTI) Building, 137–39
classes: of 1923–26, 38; of 1934, 125; of 1936, 102; of 1938, 87; of 1955, 6; of 1976, 12; of 1977, 69; of 1978, 87; of 1980, 27; of 1983, 31
Clements, Rita Crocker, 72
Clinical Sciences Building, 53
Coast Guard, 94
Coke, Gov. Richard, 62
Coke Building, 62–63
College Hospital, 65, 69, 79
College Station, 41, 42, 129, 133
Commandant of Cadets, 107
commissary, 55
Common Denominator snack bar, 110
Commons, 109–10
Computer Science, Dept. of, 131
Computer Science and Aerospace Research Building, 131–32
Computing Services Center, 113
Concrete Materials Laboratory, 133
Connally, Tom, 118
Coppini, Pompeo, 87
Corps Dorm Area, 98
Corps of Cadets, 17, 93–94, 99, 102, 108
Corps Plaza, 98
Corregidor, Philippines, 18, 72–73
Cotton Laboratory, 55
Crawford, Charles W., 78
Creamery Building (old), 116
Crocker, Pvt. Norman G., 73

Cushing, Col. E. B., 160
Cushing Library, 155, 160–61
Cyclotron, 141
Cyclotron Institute, 141

Dairy Sciences Building, 116
Dallas, 27
Dallas Times-Herald, 99
Data Processing Center, 113
Davis, Maj. Clarence R., 72
Dean of Faculties, 62
Dean of the College, first, 62
Design Institute, 143
Development Foundation, 8, 108
DeWare, Charles A., 31
DeWare Field House, 26, 31
di Cosemo, Piero, 16
Distinguished Alumni, 5. See also individual names
Dixie Classic, 27
Doherty, W. T., 135–37
Doherty Building, 135–37
Downs, P. L. ("Pinkie"), 32
Downs Natatorium, 31
drill field, 107
Duncan, William Adam, 75, 102–103
Duncan Dining Hall, 99, 102–104, 107
Duncan Field, 106
Dunn, Col. Richard J., 16, 104
Dunn, J. Harold, 110
Dunn Hall, 110
Dyke, Dr. James P., 155

East Kyle, 29
Education, College of, 81, 97
Egyptian mummy, 129
Electrical Engineering, Dept. of, 82
Electrical Engineering Building, 7, 82

El Greco, 16
Eller, David G., 121
Eller Building, 121
Engineering, College of, 78, 132, 139
Engineering and Research Center, 132
Engineering Building, 153–54
Engineering Building (old), 152
Engineering Design Graphics, 137, 154
Engineering/Physics Building, 141–43, 146
Engineers' Library, 155
English, Dept. of, 80, 101, 146
English Annex, 80
English Language Institute, 158
Entomology Research Laboratory, 55
Eppright, George, 108
eternal flame, 31
Evans Library, 53, 154–57, 160
Exchange Store, 78
Extension Service Building, 93

Facilities and Planning Office, A&M System, 148
faculty and staff homes (plaque), 10
Faculty Club, 16
Faculty Senate, 87
Faraday, Michael, 161
Farm Credit Bank, 155
Federal Land Bank, 155
Federation of Texas A&M University Mothers' Clubs, 4
Feed and Fertilizer Control Service, 148
Feed Control Division, 29
Feed Control Service, 95
Fermier, Emil Jerome, 78
Fermier Hall, 77–79, 82
Fightin' Texas Aggie Band, 101, 104

Final Review, 17
Fish Fountain, 67, 69
Flag Room, 20
Floral Test Garden, 8
Floriculture Building and Greenhouse, 115
Foley, G. ("Pat"), 12, 27
Food Engineering, 56
Food Protein Center, 56
Food Protein Research and Development Center, 56
Food Science and Technology, Dept. of, 56
Forest Genetics Greenhouse and Laboratory, 115
Forest Science, Dept. of, 50
Forest Science Building (old), 111
Forest Science laboratory, 55
Forsyth Alumni Center, 3
Fortune Cookie, The, 70
Forum, 16
Foster Hall, 76
Fountain, Charles P., 101
fountain plaza, 80
Fowler, Lt. Thomas W., 72
Francis, Dr. Mark, 52, 96, 152, 158
Francis Hall, 53, 153
Free Enterprise, Center for Education and Research in, 108
Friends of the Library, 156

G. Rollie White Coliseum, 24, 26
Gainer, Charles S., 101
Gallery, 20
Galveston, Texas A&M University at, 121
Gary, Lt. Arthur E., 72
Gathright, Thomas S., 77
Gathright Hall, 77
Gehrig, Lou, 33
General Land Office, 13

Geology Building, 129, 143
Geosciences, College of, 121
Geosciences Building, 143
Gideon, Samuel E., 83
Giesecke, Frederick Ernst, 84, 89, 122
Gill, E. King, 27
Golf Course and Clubhouse, 113
Goodwin, Charles Iverson, 90
Goodwin Hall, 89–90
Graduate College, 113
Great Depression, 99
greenhouses, 115
Grounds Maintenance, 55
Grove, 35
Guion Hall, 75, 87

Haas, Richard E., 68
Haas Hall, 68
Halbouty, Michel T., 143
Halbouty Geosciences Building, 143–46
Haney, Col. Joe T., 107
Haney Drill Field, 107
Hansen, Henry A., 5
Hansen Fountain, 5
Harrell, William George, 101
Harrington, Henry Hill, 101
Harrington, Marion Thomas, 62, 81
Harrington Education Center, 7, 81–82
Hart, L. J., 89
Hart Hall, 89, 93, 161
Hatch Act, 95
Health Center, 65
Health, Education, and Welfare, U.S. Dept. of, 75
Heaton, Homer Lloyd, 78
Heaton Hall, 77–78
Heep, Herman F., 45, 116
Heep, Minnie Belle, 45

Heep Building, 116
Heep Center for Soil and Crop Sciences, 45, 116
Heldenfels, H. C. ("Tony"), 97
Heldenfels Hall, 97
Henderson, Robert William ("Jitterbug"), 60
Henderson Hall, 59–60
Hill, Rodney, 20
Hill, Sue, 20
Hobby, Gov. William P., 75
Hobby, Lt. Gov. William P., Jr., 75
Hobby, Oveta Culp, 75
Hobby Hall, 74
Holick, Joseph F., 104
Hollywood (tent city), 61
Horticulture and Forest Science Building, 48
Horticultural Sciences, Dept. of, 8, 80
Hotard, Joseph Clifton, 75
Hotard Hall, 75
Houston, David Franklin, 7
Houston, 50
Houston and Texas Central Railroad, 41
Houston Astros, 34
Houston Bank for Cooperatives, 155
Houston Museum of Natural Science, 129
Hughes, 2nd Lt. Lloyd D., 72
Hutchinson, Joseph M., 87
Hydromechanics Laboratory, 133

Imaging Center, 134
industrial distribution, 80
Industrial Engineering, Dept. of, 132, 154
interurban, 42
intramurals, 34

Jenkins, Arthur N., 104
Journalism, Dept. of, 148

KAMU-FM, 7, 8
KAMU-TV, 7, 8
Keathley, Sgt. George Dennis, 72
Kennedy, John F., 107
Kiest, Edwin J., 99
Kiest Hall, 99
King Ranch, 43
Kleberg, Richard M., 118
Kleberg, Robert Justus, Jr., 43–44
Kleberg Animal and Food Sciences Center, 43, 45
K-9 Corps, 31
Kommerscheidt, Germany, 101
Korean War memorial, 98
Krueger, C. C. ("Polly"), 110, 157
Krueger Hall, 109–11
Kyle, Edwin Jackson, 27, 29
Kyle Field, 25, 27–31, 33, 69

Lacy, Walter G., 101
Lamar, Mirabeau B., 123
Langford, Ernest, 66, 122, 127–29, 144
Langford Architecture Center, 127–29
Large Animal Clinic, 53
Law, Francis Marion, 61
Law Hall, 61
Learning Resources Center, 97
Learning Resources Unit, 52
Le Bun Shoppe, 70
Lechner, Walter William, 67
Lechner Hall, 67
Lechner Scholarships, 68
Legett, Judge K. K., 77
Legett Hall, 76–77
Leonard, Turney W., 101
Liberal Arts, College of, 81, 146

Liberty Bell replica, 87
Library Development Council, 108
Lindsey, John H., 104
Lindsey Building, 104, 107

McDonald, Reed, 148
McFadden, Ella C., 68
McFadden Hall, 68
McInnis, Louis Lowry, 73, 101
McNew, John Thomas Lamar, 133
McNew Engineering Laboratory, 133, 139
map of Texas, 123
Market, The, 70
mascots, 31
Materials and Construction Industry Laboratory, 132
Mathematics, Dept. of, 62, 77, 80
Mattil, Dr. Karl F., 56
Maxwell, James Clerk, 161
Meat Science Center, 45
Mechanical Engineering, Dept. of, 78
Mechanical Engineering Building, 79, 82
Mechanical Engineering Shops, 80
Medal of Honor, 19, 55, 72, 94, 101
Medical Sciences Building, 50–51
Medical Sciences Library, 50, 52
Medicine, College of, 52
Memorial Student Center, 3, 12, 18–24, 35, 36
Memorial trees, 17
Memorial University Ring Collection, 4
Mendel, Gregor, 161
Meteorology, Dept. of, 121
Metzger Gun Collection, 18

Military Sciences, School of, 17
Military Sciences Building, 93, 95, 161
Military Walk, 16, 75, 76
Milner, Robert Teague, 77
Milner Hall, 76–77
Mitchell Hall, 65, 76
modular dorms, 67, 69, 72, 74, 107–108
Moore, Joe Hiram, 8
Moore, Maj. Gen. George F., 72
Moore Communications Center, 7
Moran, Charles B., 29
mosaic of university seal, 87
Moses, Maj. Gen. Andrew, 72
Mosher, Edward J., 110
Mosher Hall, 109–10
Mosher Steel Company, 110
Mrs. Sbisa's Kitchen, 70
MSC Forsyth Center Galleries, 24
Munnerlyn, Mrs. Ford, 27

Nagle, James C., 89
Nagle Hall, 84, 88–89, 97, 133, 161
Nautical Archaeology, 154
nautical fleet, university's, 121
Neeley, Marion J., 75
Neeley Hall, 74–75
Newton, Isaac, 161
North Dorm Area, 72–74, 101
North Gate, 75

Oceanography, Dept. of, 121
Oceanography and Meteorology Building, 121
official greeter, 32
Oilseed Products Laboratory, 56
Old Main, 59, 83
Old Main Drive, 41, 59, 62, 102
Olsen, C. E. ("Pat"), 33

Olsen Field, 33–34
Olympic gold medalists, 34
109th Infantry, 13
Orth, Sarah, 123

Parents Weekend, 36
Parking Garage, Northside, 146–48
Parking Garage, Southside, 107
Pasteur, Louis, 161
Pavilion, 116, 154, 158
Penberthy, Walter Lawren, 34
Penberthy Intramural Field, 34
Peterson, L. F., 158
Peterson Building, 158
petroleum engineering buildings, 134–35, 137
Physical Education Dept., 34
Physical Plant, 55
Physics, Dept. of, 89, 95, 141
Pie Are Square, 139
Placement Center, 16, 24
Planning and Institutional Analysis, 90
Plant Pathology and Microbiology, Dept. of, 158
Plant Sciences, Dept. of, 159
Plant Sciences Building (old), 158
Plato, 161
Pointe du Hoc, France, 13
Political Science, Dept. of, 82
power and machinery laboratory, 56
Power Plant Area, 146–48
President's Endowed Scholarships, 133
President's Home, 9
president's office, 16
President's Scholarships, 68, 108
Press Building, 148
Printing Center, 148
Progressive Farmer, 96
Project House site, 6

provost, 62
Psychology Building, 93, 95, 161
Public Information, Office of, 148
Public Policy Research Laboratory, 74
Purchasing and Stores Building, 55
Purple Heart, 114
Puryear, Charles, 61
Puryear Hall, 61, 63

Quad, The, 98, 102

Radiological Safety Office, 80
Range Science, Dept. of, 118
Read, Thomas, 29
Recreation and Parks, Dept. of, 111, 152
Reed McDonald Building, 148
Regents' Annex, 34
registration, 117
Remington, Frederic, 16
Republic Corporation, 110
Research Foundation, Texas A&M, 108
Reserve Officer Training Corps (ROTC), 93
restaurants. See snack bars
Reveille, 31
Reynolds, Joe H., 51
Reynolds Medical Sciences Building, 50
Richardson, Joe C., Jr., 134–35
Richardson Building, 134–35
ring collection, A&M, 4
Rockefeler, Mrs. John D., 64
Rosenthal, E. M. ("Manny"), 45–46
Rosenthal Meat Science and Technology Center, 45, 116
Ross, Lawrence Sullivan, 87
Ross Hall, 76

Ross Statue ("Sully"), 87–88
Ross Volunteer firing squad, 88
Routt, Joe, 12
Rudder, James Earl, 8, 10, 13, 82, 108
Rudder, Margaret, 108
Rudder Auditorium, 13, 16
Rudder Exhibit Hall, 16
Rudder Theater, 16
Rudder Tower, 16, 23, 38, 56, 59, 75, 89–90, 108, 125, 161
Rudder Tower and Theater Complex, 12, 14, 75, 93
Rudder Tower Fountain, 69
Rural Sociology, Dept. of, 69
Russell, Charles M., 16
Russell, Dan, 6
Ruth, Babe, 33

San Antonio A&M Club, 110
Sanders, Sam Houston, 12
Sanders Corps of Cadets Visitor Center, 12, 99
Sanders Gun Collection, 12
Sarran, James E., 18
Sbisa, Bernard, 70, 103
Sbisa Hall, 35, 70, 74–75
Sbisa's Deli Section, 70
Schiwetz, E. M. ("Buck"), 19
Schiwetz Lounge, 19
Schuhmacher, Henry C., 73, 101
Science, College of, 97
Science and Astronautics, Committee on, 114
Scoates, Daniel, 129
Scoates Hall, 129
Sea Grant, 121
2nd Ranger Battalion, 13
Serum Laboratory, 129
Shakespeare, William, 161
Shamrock Oil and Gas Corporation, 110
Shivers, Gov. Allan, 87

Silver Taps, 87
Simpson, Ormond R., 16
Simpson Drill Field, 16, 38
Singing Cadets, 22–23
sky simulator laboratory, 127
Small Animal Clinic, 53–54
Smith, Omar, 31
Smythe, D. Port, 52
snack bars and restaurants, 18, 21, 23, 24, 45, 48, 63, 70, 110, 117, 139
Soil and Crop Sciences, Dept. of, 45, 158
Southside Apartments, 6
Southwest Conference, 34–35
Spanish-American War Memorial, 10
Special Collections, 155
Special Services Building, 69, 72
Spence, David Wendell, 99
Spence Park, 12
Spirit of Aggieland, 36
Standard Meat Company, 45
state highway department, 137
State Highway 6, 41
Steed Conditioning Laboratory, 27, 30
Stock Judging Pavilion, 116, 158
Student Activities office, 24, 117
Student Finance Center, 18
Student Financial Aid, 117
Student Life Committee, 113
Student Programs office, 18, 23
Student Publications Office, 80
Student Services office, 64
Sullivan, James, 29
Sundae School, 70
System Administration Building, 3, 95, 121–25, 127, 129

Teague, Olin E. ("Tiger"), 113
Teague Research Center, 113–14
Teague Veterans' Center, 50

tent city, 61
Texaco, 81
Texas A&M Research Foundation, 74
Texas A&M Research Park, 42
Texas A&M University System, 121
Texas Agricultural Experiment Station, 95, 96, 97, 111, 152
Texas Agricultural Experiment Station Annex, 111, 113
Texas Clipper, 121
Texas Commissioner of Agriculture, 77
Texas Engineering Experiment Station, 132
Texas Independent Producers Association, 68
Texas legislature, 50, 61, 90
Texas Poll, 74
Texas Real Estate Research Center, 146
Texas Sesquicentennial, 50
Texas state chemist's office, 148
Texas Transportation Institute, 137
Texas Veterinary Medical Center, 52
Texas Wildlife Commission, 68
Theatre Arts, Dept. of, 146
Thompson, J. R., 80
Thompson Mechanical Engineering Shops, 77, 80
Tio Taco, 70
toxicology laboratories, 55
Transportation Center, 55
Trigon, 93
Triple-A Building, 74
Turner, Henry, 119

Uncle Tom's Cabin, 63
Underground, The, 70
Underwood, Ammon, 108
University Honors Program, 87

University of Texas, 7, 105, 107
University Police, 6
University Press, 74, 104
University Research, Office of, 90
U.S.D.A. Building, 74
U.S. Post Office, 75
Utay, Joseph, 101

Veterans Affairs Committee, 114
Veterinary Hospital, 54
Veterinary Hospital (old), 53, 133, 152
Veterinary Medical Center, 52–53, 152
Veterinary Medical Diagnostic Laboratory, 55
Veterinary Medicine, College of, 52–53, 116, 152
Vietnam War memorial, 99
Visitor Information Center, 108
Visualization Laboratory, 127
Von Liebig, J., 152
von Sachs, Julius, 161
Vosper, C. S. P., 122, 151

Walker, John, 52
Walton, Thomas Otto, 73
Walton Hall, 89
War Department, 93
War Within, The, 52
Wardlaw, Frank H., 105
Wardlaw Collection of Western Art, 105
Washington, George, 161
Watt, James, 161
weather vanes, 112

well, demonstration, 137
Wells, Clyde H., 108
West Campus, 31, 41, 45, 112, 116, 158
West Gate, 56
West Gate Memorial, 38
Westminster chimes, 36
West Side Athletic Complex, 31
White, Byrd E., 101
White, George Rollie, 24, 101
Whiteley, Eli Lamar, 55, 101
Whiteley Park, 55, 101
Wichita Falls A&M Club, 31
Wildlife and Fisheries Science, Dept. of, 116
Williams, Clayton W., Jr., 3
Williams, Jack Kenny, 104
Williams Alumni Center, 3
Wilson, Woodrow, 7
Wisenbaker, Royce E., 133
Wisenbaker Engineering and Research Center, 132, 134, 139
Women's Army Corps, 75
World War I, 17, 29, 38, 61, 73, 87, 94
World War II, 12, 13, 18, 30, 55, 61, 69, 75, 89, 94, 98, 104, 114–15
WTAW, 7

yell leaders, 69
YMCA Building, 3, 18, 63–64, 102

Zachry, H. B. ("Pat"), 67, 139–41
Zachry Engineering Center, 139–41